Internship
SUCCESS

Internship
SUCCESS

Real-World,
Step-by-Step
Advice on Getting
the *Most*
Out of Internships

Marianne Ehrlich Green

VGM Career Horizons
NTC/Contemporary Publishing Company

Library of Congress Cataloging-in-Publication Data

Green, Marianne Ehrlich.
    Internship success / Marianne Ehrlich Green.
       p.   cm.
    Includes bibliographical references
    ISBN 0-8442-4495-3
       1. Internship programs—United States.   2. College students—
Employment—United States.   I. Title.
    LC1072.I58G74   1997
    331.25'922—dc21   97-22902
                                             CIP

Cover design by Monica Baziuk
Interior design by Mary Lockwood

Published by VGM Career Horizons
An imprint of NTC/Contemporary Publishing Company
4255 West Touhy Avenue, Lincolnwood (Chicago), Illinois 60646-1975 U.S.A.
Copyright © 1997 by NTC/Contemporary Publishing Company
Manufactured in the United States of America
International Standard Book Number: 0-8442-4495-3

17   16   15   14   13   12   11   10   9   8   7   6   5   4   3   2

Contents

Acknowledgments

The text reflects not only the ideas and knowledge I have gathered through the years but also the suggestions, comments, and insights of my director, Dr. Edgar J. Townsend, and colleagues at the Career Services Center at the University of Delaware. I am especially grateful for the encouragement and words of wisdom offered by Dr. Richard Sharf from the Center for Counseling and Student Development. To John Green, Lauren Ehrlich, and Tobie Heller—heartfelt thanks for your unflagging support.

Preface

The word is out that internships offer high school and college students a foolproof way to get a head start in the search for employment and career success. It is my belief that *Internship Success* will spread the word about how to land great internships and make them pay great dividends. I wrote this book in response to the many questions students, faculty, administrators, and parents have raised with me through the years about the nuts and bolts of the internship experience.

Most books on the subject of internships focus on national listings of prospective internship sites. This guidebook, in contrast, addresses interns' ongoing concerns and dilemmas, such as: What's the best way to ask about payment or credit for my internship? How do I ask my supervisor for a more challenging assignment? What should I do if I experience sexual harassment at work? What typical emotional reactions do interns have and how can I best handle my feelings? How do I make my supervisor and coworkers members of my network? Questions such as these call for in-depth advice in dealing with all facets of the internship process.

For some of you, taking on an internship will give you your first contact with a professional work environment, a world at odds with lifeguarding, pizza delivery, bartending, and other survival jobs that are the financial lifeblood of most students. Making use of the suggestions and tips in *Internship Success* may help you avoid some of the pitfalls and move more smoothly into professional environments after graduation.

All the stories, incidents, cases, and scenarios found on the following pages really happened. They were related to me or to my colleagues during individual interviews or during group discussions in an experiential education seminar. I have tried to accurately recall and report the advice, suggestions, solutions, and techniques offered here. *Internship Success* includes recommendations, tips, and pointers that have proved consistently useful when applied to real-life situations. I believe this book will fill a need for both prospective and active interns in a variety of academic and employment settings across the country and around the world.

Internship
SUCCESS

1

Internships in the 1990s and Beyond

"Nothing ever

becomes **real** until

it is **experienced."**

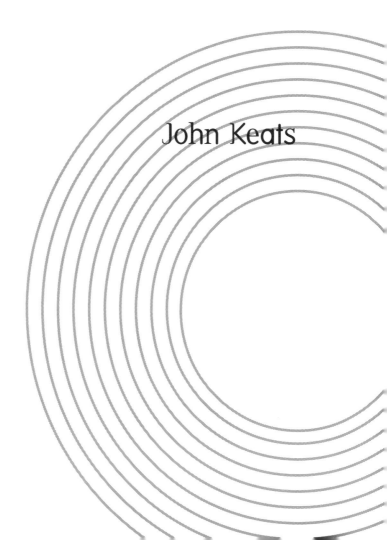

John Keats

The Internship-Job Connection

How do college students spell success in today's job market? I·N·T·E·R·N·S·H·I·P·S! Campus recruiters, professors, career counselors, and professionals from every career field recognize that academically oriented work experience provides newly minted college graduates the tools they need to compete effectively in today's tight job market. Students savvy enough to have a few internships under their belts at graduation get more interviews and field more job offers than those who fail to act on the link between career-related experience and future job prospects.

In a recent survey, May 1993 graduates of San Francisco State University cited internships as a key factor in helping them land full-time jobs (Brougham and Casella). Fifty-six percent of respondents reported the skills and work behaviors they developed as interns and volunteers were critical factors in attracting employers.

Three thousand U.S. employers surveyed by the National Center on the Educational Quality of the Workforce, in conjunction with the Bureau of the Census, also listed student internships and other work experiences as important criteria for selecting entry-level hires (*EQW National Employer Survey*, 1995). This 1995 study indicated that employers show a definite preference for job candidates whose resumes reflect related skills and hands-on knowledge in their fields.

The internship and job connection should be no surprise to you—a student of the 1990s. You know internships can contribute to your career development by helping you select a career direction and exposing you to new environments and activities. What may be less certain, however, is how to find out about your school's internship program, identify the most beneficial internships for you, initiate contact with internship supervisors, interview successfully, and make the most of your internship experiences. *Internship Success* will give you the guidance you need to become a successful graduate who can parlay internships into jobs.

Case in
Point

Colette, an economics major at a large university, reached her junior year in college with a work history that included jobs as a waitress, lifeguard, and camp counselor. She was considering a career as an economic forecaster, a business journalist, or a market researcher. Despite good grades, she knew she needed hands-on experience to help her make a decision about which field to enter, and relevant skills to convince an employer she had something to contribute beyond book knowledge. Like many students, however, Colette didn't know the logistics for hooking up with her school's internship program or finding the information and tools she needed to pursue internship options. Never having worked in a professional environment, she lacked confidence in her interpersonal skills. She knew the opportunities were out there but didn't have a clue how to take effective action.

Internships and Their Near Relations

The word *internship* usually refers to real-world work experience where students take on temporary roles as workers in an organization and reflect on these experiences in an academic setting. Internships are a new spin on the old concept of learning by doing, which has been around since the first hunter-gatherers passed on their skills to young tribal members 30,000 years ago.

Mixing theory with practice has been one of the cornerstones of American higher education for nearly 150 years (Little, p. 2). Academic programs in agriculture, engineering, teaching, medicine, and theology have offered strong hands-on components since the

9

end of the nineteenth century. More recently, some liberal arts faculty have jumped on the bandwagon, convinced that relevant work experience plus a strong generalist background provide the winning combination to ensure job success for liberal arts majors.

Programs that integrate academic and real-world experience have sprung up—almost overnight—on many high school and college campuses. They are called by a variety of names: cooperative education, field experience, service learning, field work, practicums, externships, and apprenticeships. Distinctions among these experiential programs tend to blur when they are examined closely. What is called an internship in one setting may be referred to as field experience or cooperative education in another. It quickly becomes evident that each of these terms is defined and applied differently depending on the school and its faculty.

Internship. This term is often used generically to refer to any temporary work experience, in a for-profit or nonprofit setting, with the dual purpose of learning while working. Internships can be integrated with the student's regular school schedule or take place during a semester away from school or during the summer break. They can involve academic credit or remuneration. Some internships have an academic component and a faculty sponsor. Internship models may vary from school to school and even among departments on campus. Terminology also may vary: *Internship* may be used interchangeably with *field experience* or *co-op* to describe programs that look similar, or strikingly different. Because of the confusion of program models and terms, you may run into difficulty sorting out the different programs offered by each school.

Cooperative Education (co-op). Derived from a relationship of cooperation between school and employer, co-op can refer to an institutional mandatory program or to a departmental elective program. In the majority of co-op programs, students work full time for pay in business or industry for one or more semesters, alternating with full-time classroom study. Other types of co-op programs run parallel to regular academic schedules and carry academic credit. In some cases, college graduation must be extended beyond the typical four years to accommodate time spent on the job. Historically, only departments of engineering, business, and science sponsored co-op programs, but today co-op has become a popular option in many other departments as well.

Drexel University in Philadelphia, Antioch College in Yellow Springs, Ohio, and Northeastern University in Boston exemplify co-op schools—colleges that provide mandatory, off-campus work experience for the majority of students. At present, cooperative education programs exist on more than one thousand college campuses across the United States. For additional information, consult the *Co-op Education Undergraduate Program Directory* available from the National Commission for Cooperative Education, 360 Huntington Ave., Boston, MA 02115.

Service Learning, Field Experience, and Volunteer Work. These terms usually refer to unpaid work in the human services or nonprofit sector, running parallel to the student's regular class schedule. Students in these programs select sites that make a contribution to meeting the needs of the community. A credit-bearing class or written report are often part of this type of experiential program. Evaluations from site supervisors plus academic work usually determine grades. Listings of local service-learning and field-experience opportunities may be available at your college's career services office or through an academic department's volunteer coordinator. On some campuses, local volunteer, field-experience, and service-learning opportunities are promoted at volunteer fairs or expos where representatives from various community organizations recruit students to participate in activities within their agencies.

Externships, Mentoring, and Shadowing Programs. Short-term placements in various worksites for purposes of observation and information gathering usually fall under these program titles. Alumni are often willing to provide students who share an interest in their careers with opportunities to conduct information interviews and observe daily activities in their places of employment. For many students, these exploratory programs lead to full-blown internships or co-ops at a later date.

Apprenticeships. Traditionally, this term has been applied to a method of learning a trade or skill by working directly with a master of the craft. Academic learning components are not usually associated with apprenticeship programs. Individual schools, however, sometimes redefine the term so their apprenticeships are similar to typical internship programs. More information about traditional apprenticeships is available from the Bureau of Apprenticeship and Training, a division of the United States Department of Labor.

College Work-Study Program. This federally funded program allows eligible students with financial need to take jobs on campus, or in some cases, off campus. The federal government contributes approximately 70 percent of student wages and the rest is picked up by the college. Tasks typically include clerical work, manual labor, food service, library work, and basic administrative functions. If nonprofit organizations have contracts with the college work-study office, eligible students who work or intern for them off campus can be paid with work-study funds. If you think you qualify for work-study funds, visit the financial aid office on your campus for further information.

All these common terms for academically oriented work experience—internships, co-op, field experience, service learning, practicums, volunteer work, apprenticeships, externships, etc.—are subject to definition and interpretation by the college you attend or the program you wish to enter. In fact, some internships are indistinguishable from part-time or summer jobs. Eligibility requirements for participating in internships also vary from program to program. Some internships are open only to full-time students enrolled at a certain educational institution. Others may be available to high school students, recent college graduates, career changers, or senior citizens.

No matter what you call them, these programs can supply the hands-on experience you need to compete effectively for full-time positions. Take time to investigate internships and related opportunities offered by your school to determine which best meet your needs. For additional information, contact the National Society for Experiential Education (NSEE), 3509 Haworth Dr., Ste. 207, Raleigh, NC 27609.

Internships Pay Off for Employers

Companies definitely do not employ interns solely out of the goodness of their hearts. Interns are primarily a source of inexpensive or free labor in times of cutbacks and layoffs. Many organizations, particularly nonprofits, depend on interns to supply needed help in clerical, programmatic, and administrative areas. One executive director of a health care organization summed up this fact of life: "Without my two interns, our community projects in the mall would come to a crashing halt. I just don't have the paid staff to do everything that needs to get done."

Internship programs also provide a pool for recruiting full-time employees. New hires are frequently drawn from the ranks of former interns whose work behavior and skills have already been put to the test. It makes sense that interns who have proved themselves to a company throughout a semester of successful on-the-job experience will be favored candidates for full-time positions. Many college career centers have noted that a number of technical companies show more interest in receiving undergraduate resumes and scheduling summer internships than in recruiting graduating seniors. "More and more companies see the summer internship as a cost-effective way to groom future candidates for full-time positions while weeding out the misfits," says Dave Berilla, employer relations associate director for the University of Delaware.

Further, internship programs tend to build firm bridges between academia and the surrounding community. Cross-fertilization of resources and ideas benefits schools, businesses, and community agencies. Community leaders and board members often credit participation in their schools' volunteer projects, service-learning, and internship programs for planting the seeds of their lifetime commitment to making a difference to their communities and their country.

II

Landing the Best Internship for You

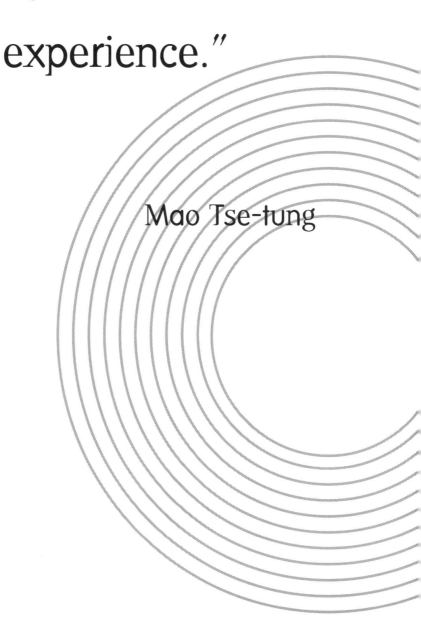

"All genuine **knowledge**

originates from direct

experience."

Mao Tse-tung

Scoping Out Great Internships

A little detective work will uncover almost unlimited internship possibilities. Explore the numerous avenues available to find the internship that's right for you.

■ Use your campus telephone directory to identify co-op or internship offices on campus. Many schools have specially trained staff to help students with internship concerns.

■ Make an appointment with your advisor, guidance counselor, or department chair to find out about internship options connected with your field of study.

■ Locate your school's career services office and library; there may be an internship coordinator on staff. Most career libraries have extensive listings of local organizations that are looking for interns. Descriptions of these internships are commonly posted, collected in notebooks, filed, or entered into a database. Ask to see if your school's career office has a handout that summarizes procedures for identifying and pursuing internships.

Career libraries also have copies of association publications, newsletters, brochures, and directories of internships for every possible field in locations across the United States and around the world.

■ Build your own list of local, regional, national, or international organizations that might have an internship for you. Use the chamber of commerce directory from your target city, the local yellow pages, or national directories such as the *Standard Directory of Advertising Agencies*, *International Directory of Marketing Research Companies*, or *Insurance Phone Book and Directory*. The organizations you contact may not consider employing an intern until you bring up the topic. Many enterprising students have arranged extraordinary internships by making the initial contact themselves.

■ If you have access to the Internet, use a search engine such as Alta Vista or Yahoo to explore entries with *internship* as the key word. The Internet lists hundreds of internship sites, and many organizations have web pages that provide an excellent resource for researching potential internships.

The following internship directories, found in many university and public libraries, will start you in the right direction.

Resources for Finding Internships

International Internships and Volunteer Programs
Will Cantrell and Francine Modderno
Cantrell Corporation, 1992

Internships
Sara Dulaney Gilbert
Macmillan, 1995

6th Annual Graduate Group's Internships:
    State and Federal Government
The Graduate Group, 1994–95

The National Directory of Arts Internships
Warren Christensen
The National Network for Artist Placement, 1993–94

The National Directory of Internships, 1996 edition
Gila Gulati and Nancy Bailey, editors
National Society for Internships and Experiential
    Education, 1995

America's Top 100 Internships
Mark Oldman and Samer Hamaden
Willard Books, 1996

Peterson's Internships 1996
Peterson's, 1995

InternAmerica
(An internship newsletter published by
    Bernard Ford)
105 Chestnut St., Ste. 34
Needham, MA 02192

The Facts of the Matter

How Internship Programs Work

Find out as much as you can about the rules and regulations governing your high school or college internship program. Some internships may require that you receive academic credit. Others may have a list of approved sites to choose from. Ask your school's internship coordinator, guidance counselor, co-op advisor, or department chair the following questions *before* you contact potential internship sites:

- Where can I get a written description of my school's internship program?

- Is there a list of recommended internships related to my field of interest?

■ How many internship hours must I complete during the semester, summer, or intersession?

■ Who will evaluate my internship performance?

■ Will I receive credit or a grade for my internship?

■ Do I arrange my own internship or will someone else make the initial contact for me?

■ Is this internship parallel (integrated with my regularly scheduled classes) or alternating (full-time work)?

■ Does the internship involve learning contracts—documents in which the internship participant, employer, and sponsor acknowledge agreed-upon objectives? (See Example 1 on pages 35–36.)

■ Can I expect an on-site visit from a faculty sponsor?

■ Does a required class or seminar accompany my internship? Will I have projects, assignments, papers, or presentations to complete?

■ Will I receive a stipend, reimbursement for expenses, or an hourly wage?

■ Must I sign a waiver absolving my school of responsibility if I am injured while at my internship site? (See Example 2 on page 37.)

■ What transportation arrangements must I make?

What's in It for You?

Setting Your Internship Goals

There is no shortage of internship opportunities out there. Most employers are eager to test potential employees while using their skills. Your time is limited, however, and you may not have the opportunity to pursue more than one internship. How do you pick the internship that is best for you—one that will help you develop career-related experience and knowledge as well as contacts for your future job search?

To identify the best internship for you, it helps to first figure out what you want to gain from the internship experience. Be specific about what you hope to learn and how you wish to be enriched by your experiences. Above and beyond enhancing your resume with career-related experience and building contacts for a future job search, there are other valuable goals your internship can help you attain.

■ **Learn more about a chosen industry or field, such as:** financial services, insurance, retail, transportation, real estate, manufacturing, cultural organizations, communications or media, education, health care, entertainment, recreation, religious or volunteer organizations, and government.

Case in Point

Jake's long-range goal was to become a judge, but he had no experience in the legal field. He secured an internship working at family court—attending court sessions and observing lawyers and judges. His experiences helped confirm his interest in the legal profession.

■ **Apply classroom theory to real-life situations.**

Case in
Point

In accordance with behavioral theories she learned in psychology class, Dana was interested in using positive reinforcement such as M&Ms candies to assist in teaching autistic children. She interned at a program for autistic children to see this strategy in action.

■ **Become more knowledgeable about general work functions, such as:** *marketing* (market research, product management, advertising, and promotion); *human resources* (training, safety, recruitment, equal opportunity, benefits, labor relations); *communications* (customer relations, government relations, investor relations, employee communications, community relations, creative services); *operations* (manufacturing, shipping, purchasing, maintenance, security, travel, contract administration); *finance* (cash management, credit, collections, long-range budgeting, pensions, tax management, mergers and acquisitions, accounting); and *research and development* (pure research, product quality control, product engineering, new product development).

Case in Point

Drew wanted to use his psychology background for a career in human resources. He looked for an internship that would allow him to learn about all human resource functions, especially training and development. His sister, Myra, focused on an internship where she could use her accounting background in the financial function of a hospital, school, religious organization, or business.

■ **Investigate organizational culture**—the unwritten rules, power structure, assumptions, degree of formality, dress codes, communication styles, and rituals characteristic of a particular workplace. For many people, the workplace environment holds the key to satisfying employment.

Case in Point

Marti had worked summers in a business environment but disliked the focus on money and the cutthroat atmosphere. She wanted an internship that would give her the chance to work in a nonprofit environment where she hoped to find a "kinder and gentler" culture.

■ **Learn career-related skills**—abilities directly related to job responsibilities, such as: public speaking, writing articles and reports, editing, interviewing, promoting events, dealing with customers, researching, analyzing data, selling, using the computer, coordinating events, advising, budgeting, handling complaints, interpreting languages, administering programs, instructing, designing, presenting, marketing, selling, rehabilitating.

Case in
Point

Bree knew her English literature major would not convince an advertising agency she could copyedit. She sought an internship that would augment her editing skills and give her the chance to prepare samples to interest future employers.

■ **Perform a positive service for the community.**

Case in

Point

Making a difference for people who are physically challenged was an important consideration for Paul when he looked for an internship. Though his major was business administration, he wanted to work in a setting where his contribution might add to the quality of other people's lives. He eventually selected an internship site in the accounting office of a rehabilitation hospital.

Polish communication skills needed in the workplace, such as: listening, questioning, confronting, giving and receiving feedback, dealing with criticism and praise. Gain valuable experience dealing with different communication styles that arise from cultural, gender, and power differences among employees.

Case in

Point

From personal experience, Jeremy knew he needed to practice asking questions in the workplace. His reluctance to speak up and clarify his supervisor's instructions during a previous summer job had resulted in his making a serious mistake. Now Jeremy wanted to use his internship opportunity at a research facility to practice and enhance his ability to communicate effectively with supervisors and other authority figures.

■ **Other goals?**

_____

_____

_____

The more specific you are about your internship goals, the easier it will be to evaluate prospective internships to determine which will deliver the greatest return for your involvement. It is certainly possible and advisable to have more than one goal. A good internship will allow you to meet multiple goals. Just take the time to think through, write down, and be able to articulate what you would like to accomplish in the course of your internship. You must share the responsibility for a poor internship experience if you fail to define your goals and seek out a suitable internship under the direction of a supervisor who supports those goals.

Many internship programs require that a learning contract, spelling out your internship goals and appropriate activities to meet those goals, be signed by you and your internship supervisor. Identifying specific learning goals can help in preparing this document and can provide a focus for periodic assessment and final evaluation of your internship experience. (See Example 1.)

(Example 1)

Learning Contract
Internship Program
Career Services Center

Section I—Student Identification

Name _____Social Security #_____

Student Address _____

Permanent Address _____

Campus Telephone # _____

Home Telephone #_____

Major_____College _____

Class Standing F_____ So _____ J_____ Sr_____

Section II—Internship Description

Position Title_____Supervisor's Name _____

Supervisor's Signature _____

Title _____

Agency Name _____

Dates of Assignment _____ to _____Hours per week_____

Agency Telephone #_____

Brief Description of Intern Responsibilities: _____

_____

_____

_____

_____

Section III—Goal Statement

Describe primary goals and objectives to be accomplished by your field experience:

_____

_____

_____

_____

_____

Section IV—Approval Signatures

Student _____Date_____

Advisor, Field Experience Program _____

Date _____

(Example 2)
Waiver and Release of Liability Agreement

Name of Activity _____

Name of Participant _____Age _____

Address _____Phone_____

City, State, Zip_____Date of Birth _____

I,_____, acknowledge that I have voluntarily chosen to participate in the above-referenced activity and have full knowledge of the risks this activity presents, including travel to, participation in, and returning from the activity.

I understand that by being permitted to participate in this activity, I agree to assume any and all risk of injury or death. I further understand and agree to assume responsibility for all risk of theft, loss, or damage of personal property that occurs at any time arising out of my participation in the activity.

I understand and agree that as a condition of participation in the activity, i further agree to release from liability and to indemnify the University of_____, and its officers, directors, agents, employees, assigns, successors, or lessors for any damage, injury, or death to myself or to any person or property in any way connected with my participation in the activity.

I understand and agree that I have carefully read this agreement and fully understand all its terms and conditions. I understand that this is a release of liability that could legally prevent me from filing suit or making any other legal claim for damages in the event of my death or injury to me. With this knowledge, I am entering into this agreement freely and voluntarily. I agree that it is binding upon me, my spouse, my heirs, my children, including any guardian ad litem for the children, my assigns, and legal representatives.

I understand and agree that if I am signing this waiver and release on behalf of my minor child, I will be giving up the same rights for the minor as I would be giving up if I signed this document on my own behalf.

I understand and agree that I have read this waiver and release, have provided all necessary information, and have signed in the appropriate places.

Date_____Signature _____

What Do *You* Bring to the Table?

Self-Assessment

After determining what you want to get out of your internship, your next step is to figure out what you can put into the internship. Employers are usually eager to expose you to their work environment and show you the ropes, but they also expect a contribution from you. What do you have to offer? What skills and abilities do you currently have? These questions may be asked at an interview. Even though you probably lack specific experience and knowledge of the organization for which you would like to intern and its day-to-day operations, your years as a student, part-time worker, and volunteer have certainly given you a repertoire of practical skills that could prove beneficial.

Check off the skills and traits you already possess and try to think of situations in which you demonstrated them.

☐ technical skills—basic knowledge of personal or mainframe computers, word processing or spreadsheet software, and desktop publishing packages

☐ clerical skills

☐ facility with office equipment

☐ communication skills—writing, public speaking, instructing

☐ artistic skills—designing flyers, posters, logos

☐ organizational skills—coordinating, managing, administering

☐ foreign language skills

☐ positive attitude—enthusiasm, willingness to tackle any task, eagerness to learn

☐ good work behavior—punctuality, ability to meet deadlines, careful attention to detail

☐ other

An important part of self–assessment is identifying your limitations as well as your strengths. Transportation difficulties, age or educational constraints, financial considerations, time availability, lack of credit opportunities, internship requirements, and other possible conflicts will determine which internships you can realistically pursue. Don't make commitments you aren't sure you can keep.

Case in Point

A summer internship at a major television station in New York looked very appealing to Sean, a communications major. He had to evaluate his financial situation, however, to see if he could afford to live in New York and take an unpaid internship for three months. Ultimately, he had to settle for a less prestigious local television station so he could maintain his part-time job and live at home.

Getting It Together

Preparing Your Resume

One of the best internship search tools at your disposal is your resume. While not all internship sites require resumes from prospective interns, it is better to be on the safe side and have one ready for inspection. It is awkward and unprofessional to respond negatively to a request for your resume.

Most career services offices offer workshops on resume writing, as well as opportunities to have your resume critiqued. Your department advisor or interested professors are usually willing to give tips on the subject. There is also a plethora of books on resume preparation available in school and community libraries, at most bookstores, and in your career services office. Key points to remember as you put together this important marketing tool are:

- Be brief. A resume longer than one page may strike employers as puffery.

- Be accurate. An error-free resume communicates your attention to detail and your organizational skills in a powerful way.

- Stress your accomplishments. Use action verbs, examples, and numbers to demonstrate your abilities and quantify your accomplishments.

Case in Point

Marla found the perfect internship through her career services office and telephoned the contact person to see if she could make an appointment to discuss the opportunity. Marla's contact asked her to send her resume as soon as possible. Since Marla hadn't yet prepared a resume, she had to do a rush job, resulting in a document that inadequately represented her accomplishments and arrived late at the internship site.

(Example 3)

Sample Resume

Judith A. Madeira

Local address	**Permanent Address**
341 S. Elm	530 King Street
St. Louis, MO 63130	Clayton, MO 63102
(314) 555-7373	(314) 555-1739

Objective

To obtain a summer internship in the public relations field.

Education

Bachelor of Arts in Sociology, Washington University, St. Louis, MO (expected May 1997). Minor: Women's Studies. GPA 3.1/4.0. Dean's List, two semesters.

High School Diploma, Clayton High School, Clayton, MO (May 1993). Received Dad's Club Scholarship.

Experience

Lifeguard, Miller's Pool, Clayton, MO (Summer 1994, 1993)
Spearheaded campaign to ensure safe diving techniques. Produced posters and pamphlets that were distributed to swim clubs around the state. Maintained pool safety standards.

Salesperson, Hallmark Card Shop, Kirkwood, MO (Summer 1992)
Sold cards and gifts to more than 300 customers per week. Received two "Employee of the Week" awards.

Waitress, The Bell Ringer, Olivette, MO (Summer 1991)

Activities

President, Equestrian Club (1995)
Membership Chair (1994)
Planned "Ride Home for Charlie," a countywide fund-raiser involving more than 200 participants and their horses. Raised $2,000 for a hospitalized student. Designed, produced, and distributed publicity for this event.
Member, swim team (1993–94)
Editor, Clayton High School yearbook (1992–93)

Skills and Awards

- Knowledge of Print Shop, PageMaker, and WordPerfect 6.0 for Windows. Familiar with Macs, PCs, and mainframes.
- Placed second in Lion's Club public speaking contest (1993).

Resources for Writing Resumes

The Adams Resume Almanac
Robert Adams
Bob Adams, Inc. 1994

The Resume Makeover
Jeffrey G. Allen
John Wiley & Sons, 1995

The Complete Resume Guide
Marian Faux
Macmillan, 1996

Trashproof Resumes
Timothy D. Haft
Random House, 1995

Perfect Resume Strategies
Tom and Ellen Jackson
Doubleday, 1992

Electronic Resume Revolution
Joyce Lain Kennedy and Thomas Morrow
John Wiley & Sons, 1994

The Best Resumes for Scientists and Engineers
Adele Lewis
John Wiley & Sons, 1988

Strategic Resumes
Marcis Mahoney
Crisp Publications, 1994

The College Student Resume Guide
Kim Marino
Ten Speed Press, 1992

Resumes Made Easy
Patty Marler and Jan Bailey Mattia
VGM Career Horizons, 1995

How to Write a Winning Resume
Deborah Perlmutter Bloch, Ph.D.
VGM Career Horizons, 1993

The Guide to Basic Resume Writing
Public Library Association Job and Career
    Information Services Committee
VGM Career Horizons, 1991

Slam Dunk Resumes
Steven Provenzano
VGM Career Horizons, 1994

Making Contact with Employers

Once you have clarified your school's internship rules and regulations, set realistic goals, assessed your strengths and limitations, and prepared a resume, it's time to put together a prospect list of internship sites and begin to make contact. In some cases, your initial contact with employers will be made by a professor, an internship coordinator, or another individual. In most cases, however, you will be responsible for making the contact yourself, by either calling a prospective internship site or sending your resume with an accompanying cover letter.

Contacting an Organization
Seeking Interns

*"Mr. Johnson, my name is Brian James and I am an account-
ing major at the University of Delaware. I would like to speak
to you about an internship with Miles, Inc., for the fall 1996
semester."*

    *"Hello, this is Susan Peterman calling about the internship
with family court that your agency listed in the field experience
notebooks in the career resource center at the University of
Delaware."*

Cold Calling

*"Hello, Dr. Eddy, I am a psychology major at the university. Pro-
fessor Alan Diamond suggested I call you to discuss an internship under your direction at the state hospital."*

    *"I read about an internship with the American Cancer Soci-
ety in the* National Internship Directory *and am calling to
get more information about this opportunity. My name is Kevin
Monahan and I am a student at Bradley University."*

    *"Hello. Would you connect me with the person at Majors
Laboratory who deals with interns? There isn't anyone with
that responsibility? Could you refer me to the appropriate person who could give me information about internships in ani-
mal research? I am a biology major at the University of
Delaware, and I'm very interested in a summer internship with
your organization."*

Sending a Compelling Letter

A cover letter (see Examples 4 and 5 on pages 52 and 53) is an important tool in the internship search and should be mailed with the resume. It is optional, however, when you deliver a resume in person. Information on writing cover letters is available at the career services office at your school, at local bookstores, and in all libraries. Five things to remember when writing cover letters are:

1. Avoid standardized or form letters.
2. Address the letter to a specific person.
3. Limit the letter to three paragraphs. In the first, state the purpose of the letter. In the second, offer three selling points with reference to your resume. In the final paragraph, request an interview.
4. Limit the letter to one page.
5. Keep the letter error free.

(Example 4)

Cover Letter

January 3, 1996

452 Briar Lane
Newark, DE 19711

Ms. Meredith Vickers
March of Dimes, Inc.
420 Schoolhouse Lane
Wilmington, DE 19808

Dear Ms. Vickers:

As a communications major at the University of Delaware, I am very interested in the public relations field. After reading a brochure about your organization in our career library, I decided an internship with the March of Dimes would give me the chance to apply my background in oral and written communications as well as learn a great deal about my field of interest.

My enclosed resume indicates I have some experience with PageMaker and Print Shop, skills that could be useful in developing newsletters, brochures, and advertisements. I believe my fund-raising background would also help me contribute to your Spring Flower Fair. My excellent grades during the past two years should show you I am a hard worker and a quick learner.

I am available after 3:00 P.M. on Wednesday, Thursday, or Friday afternoons for an interview to discuss a semester-long internship with the March of Dimes. I appreciate your time and consideration and look forward to hearing from you soon.

Sincerely,

Jamie Stevens
555-0957

Enclosure: resume

(Example 5)

Cover Letter

March 5, 1996

42 Madison Road
Baltimore, MD 21204

Mr. Steven Vanzetti
Thornton, Inc.
New Richmond, CT 54322

Dear Mr. Vanzetti:

When I called Thornton on December 4, 1995, your secretary, Ms. Angel, suggested I contact you about the possibility of obtaining an internship with your organization for the summer of 1996. I am an excellent student, have some sales experience, and am eager to learn more about the pharmaceutical industry.

As my enclosed resume indicates, I have worked for two years in the advertising sales department of the *Review*, my college newspaper, which has a circulation of 20,000. During that time, I increased the number of companies who advertise in the *Review* by 25 percent. In addition, I was vice president of the Outing Club and organized and coordinated three cross-country ski trips which involved 100 students and more than $10,000. These abilities, combined with a 3.4 grade point average in my marketing major, would help me contribute to your organization while learning more about the pharmaceutical industry.

An interview would allow me to provide additional information in person; I will be available to meet with you any afternoon after 2:00 P.M. Thank you for considering me as a potential intern at Thornton.

Sincerely,

Marla S. Gilpin
201-555-7373

Enclosure: resume

Resources for Writing Cover Letters

The Perfect Cover Letter
Richard H. Beatty
John Wiley & Sons, 1989

175 High Impact Cover Letters
Richard H. Beatty
John Wiley & Sons, 1992

The National Business Employment Weekly: Cover Letters
Taunee Besson
John Wiley & Sons, 1995

Letters for Job Hunters
William S. Frank
Ten Speed Press, 1990

Dynamic Cover Letters
Katharine Hansen with Randall Hansen
Ten Speed Press, 1992

Job Search Letters That Get Results
Ronald Krannich and Caryl Rae Krannich
Impact Publications, 1992

How to Write Successful Cover Letters
Karyn E. Langhorne and Eric R. Martin
VGM Career Horizons, 1994

Cover Letters They Don't Forget
Eric Martin and Karyn E. Langhorne
VGM Career Horizons, 1993

Job Choices: 1996
Edited by the National Association of Colleges
    and Employers
NACE, 1995

The Guide to Basic Cover Letter Writing
Public Library Association Job and Career
    Information Services Committee
VGM Career Horizons, 1995

Slam Dunk Cover Letters
Mark Rowh
VGM Career Horizons, 1997

Preparing for the Internship Interview

The interview is the single most important factor in landing an internship. Good resumes, cover letters, and telephone conversations can get you in the door, but structured, face-to-face interaction is required before hiring decisions can be made.

Preparation is definitely the key to successful interviewing. Taking time to prepare can increase the odds that you will make a favorable impression.

■ Demonstrate a positive attitude. An enthusiastic candidate who seems eager to learn, gets along with others, and goes the extra mile will always be in demand.

■ Indicate clear learning goals. Do you want to learn more about interpersonal communication, organizational types and cultures, a specific industry, one or more job functions, or career-related skills? A combination of all five? Be able to discuss relevant activities that would help you meet your internship goals.

Many internship programs require that some form of contract be signed by you and your internship supervisor so both parties have a clear understanding, in writing, of what you hope to learn during your internship. Sometimes this document must be reviewed and signed by your sponsoring professor, internship coordinator, or internship seminar leader. (See Example 1 on page 35.)

T I P

Be sure to have any required paperwork, such as a learning contract, properly filled out and ready for the interviewer's comments and signature.

■ Research the organization. Ask yourself the following questions:

■ What type organization is this—for profit, non-profit, or government?

■ What are its products or services?

■ Who uses or benefits from these products and services?

■ Who are this organization's competitors? What are its challenges?

■ Is this a thriving organization?

■ Have there been any recent articles about this organization in the news?

■ What is the organization's mission?

TIP

Read annual reports, recruitment literature, brochures, write-ups in directories such as *Standard & Poor's, Dun and Bradstreet's Career Guide,* or your city's human services directory. Use on-line search services to locate articles. Speak to former interns, friends, and professors who may know something about this organization.

■ Try to think of anecdotes, incidents, or situations to illustrate your answers to the following commonly asked interview questions:

  ■ Why do you want an internship with this particular organization?

  ■ What are your career goals?

  ■ We have several candidates for this internship position; why should we choose you?

  ■ What are your greatest strengths and your biggest weaknesses?

  ■ What type supervisor do you prefer to work with?

  ■ Who was your least favorite professor? Why?

  ■ How would you handle conflicts between your school schedule and a surprise, rush job here?

  ■ Tell me about your role in extracurricular activities? How many hours do you spend weekly on these commitments?

  ■ Is your grade point average reflective of your true ability? Why? Why not?

■ You may hear things at this site that must remain confidential. Can you give me an example of situations where you have had to observe strict confidentiality?

Questions that begin: "What would you do if . . ." or "How would you react to . . ." are designed to get an overall impression of how you might think or react in situations you could encounter during your internship. These questions are difficult to anticipate unless you have some in-depth knowledge of the organization and have talked to former interns or current employees.

TIP

Avoid talking too much or too little—answering just "yes" or "no." Don't speak negatively about other supervisors, professors, or peers. Be able to cite examples of situations where you demonstrated skills or positive personal attributes.

■ Prepare questions to ask your interviewer. For example:

■ What are some of the tasks and projects I will be involved in?

■ What are your expectations of an intern who works for your organization?

■ What is the dress code of your organization?

■ Will I have the opportunity to meet regularly with my internship supervisor?

■ What sort of training or orientation will I receive?

■ How many hours per week will you want me to work?

■ Will there be a salary or stipend for my work here?

■ Will I receive reimbursement for my travel expenses?

■ Will I be covered by workers' compensation if I am injured at my internship site?

T I P

As a general rule, avoid bringing up the subject of salary, benefits, and reimbursement. In those cases, however, where remuneration of some type has a direct bearing on whether or not you can accept the internship, it is helpful to introduce and clarify financial matters up front so you and your internship supervisor are on the same wavelength about this important subject before you proceed any further.

■ Develop a professional image. A suit is the preferred interviewing attire for both men and women. Darker colors tend to convey an air of authority that could offset a youthful appearance. Men's color choices should be limited to grays and navy blue, with or without a pinstripe. Women have a wider range of color choices but should avoid busy patterns and pastels. In most cases, however, the purchase of a new, expensive suit for an internship interview isn't necessary. A sports jacket, tie, and presentable slacks for a man and a coatdress or blazer and skirt for a woman are acceptable. Students are not expected to have a professional wardrobe.

Fine-tune the details of your appearance. Polish your shoes, groom your nails, but avoid flashy jewelry and strong scents. Practice mock interviewing with a friend or watch yourself on videotape to critique your nonverbal gestures. Jittery hand and leg movements, a weak handshake, and poor eye contact suggest lack of confidence.

TIP

Formal dress may not be normal workplace attire for a particular internship site; nevertheless, you should take special pains to look professional at your interview to show you are prepared to take your internship seriously. As an intern, your everyday attire should follow the dress code of your internship site.

■ Prepare some samples of your work to share with your interviewer. If your internship involves writing or artistic skills, bring examples of your school assignments or projects that showcase these skills. Visible proof of your abilities will effectively make the case that you would be a valuable asset to the organization.

T I P

Displaying samples of your work in a well-organized portfolio is very effective when you interview for a full-time position. Be sure to keep copies of projects from past, present, and future internships to include in your portfolio.

■ Follow up. After your internship interview, take the time to write a prompt thank–you note to the key person who interviewed you. This note can be typed on business stationery or handwritten on a card. This extra effort shows your appreciation for your interviewer's time, reiterates your interest, and reminds the interviewer why you are a good candidate for the position. (See Example 6 on the next page.)

(Example 6)
Sample Interview Thank-You Letter

September 3, 1996

4440 Bellford Drive
Newark, DE 19711

Ms. Rachel Brahms, Executive Director
United Diabetes Foundation
3828 E. Lexington Alley
Wilmington, DE 19808

Dear Ms. Brahms:

Thank you so much for taking time from your busy schedule last Friday to interview me for the internship position at the United Diabetes Foundation. After our meeting, I am convinced that your organization is the best place for me to learn about nonprofit management, my long-term career goal.

As you may remember, I have skills in desktop publishing and newswriting and would be able to write press releases as well as work on your newsletter. I was pleased by your interest in my ideas for an updated office brochure and flyer. I believe I can make a contribution to the United Diabetes Foundation while I learn as much as possible about how the organization is administered.

Please let me know if I can provide you with any additional information about my background or goals. I look forward to hearing from you soon.

Cordially,

Brian D. Linton

Resources for Interviewing Information

Preparing for Your Interview
Diane Berk
Crisp Publications, 1990

Make Your Job Interview a Success
J. I. Biegeleisen
Arco, 1994

The Professional Image
Susan Bixler
Putnam Publishing Group, 1984

How to Have a Winning Job Interview
Deborah Perlmutter Bloch, Ph.D.
VGM Career Horizons, 1992

Your First Interview
Ron Fry
Career Press, 1993

The Winning Image
James Gray
American Management Association, 1993

Dynamite Answers to Interview Questions
Caryl Rae Krannich and Ronald L. Krannich
Impact Publications, 1992

Interview for Success
Caryl Rae Krannich and Ronald L. Krannich
Impact Publications, 1993

The Complete Job Interview Handbook
John J. Marcus
Barnes and Noble, 1988

Job Interviews Made Easy
Patty Marler and Jan Bailey Mattia
VGM Career Horizons, 1995

Job Interviewing for College Students
John D. Shingleton
VGM Career Horizons, 1995

Experience: Your Best Teacher

"Experience is

not what happens to a man.

It is what a man does

with what happens to him."

Aldous Huxley

Getting the Most Out of Your Internship Experience

*A*nticipation is the first of the five predictable stages new interns typically experience in the course of their internships (Sweitzer and King). Before your first day on the job you will probably feel excited, hopeful, and anxious about the people and situations you will encounter. Your expectations will be high about what you will learn and be able to contribute. Of course, you want to take full advantage of this wonderful opportunity, especially if this is the only internship you'll be able to fit into your schedule. A case of nerves about how you'll handle new challenges, coworkers, and clients is natural. To prepare for your first day at your internship, study the following comments from employers about the qualities they look for or dislike

73

Positive Traits	Negative Traits
asks a lot of questions	fails to ask relevant questions
follows directions well	follows own agenda
understands some gofer work is part of the job	objects to routine work
displays enthusiasm	lacks energy and enthusiasm
actively looks for things to do	fails to display initiative
follows rules and regulations	disregards office rules and policies
socializes appropriately with staff	has poor interpersonal skills
exhibits punctuality and dependability	displays irresponsibility and lack of punctuality
tries to understand the organization	tries to jump in too soon without knowing the organization
checks out all projects with supervisor	fails to keep supervisor informed about activities

in interns. Try to model the positive traits to increase the odds your internship will meet your expectations.

In order to obtain maximum benefit from your internship, it makes sense to plan an ongoing method for reflecting on your experiences. Raw experience leads to learning only when it is processed and organized in a structured way (Kolb). Reflection takes you beyond merely observing the daily events that occur at your internship or simply completing your assigned tasks and duties. Reflection involves interpreting, analyzing, speculating, evaluating, comparing, contrasting, discovering, weighing, recognizing, and remembering. Prior to beginning your internship, your internship coordinator, faculty sponsor, or supervisor may assign you a formal scheme for internship reflection, or you could choose one on your own. No matter which method you use, you will find that reflection is vital in meeting your internship goals.

Journal or Log. This is one of the most frequently prescribed methods for reflecting on internship experiences. Unless you are specifically directed to use a particular style of notebook, plan on a light-weight, transportable journal you can carry to and from your internship. You can use it to jot down phrases, quotes, and key words to help you remember what transpires during the day. Later, record the sequence of daily events as well as unusual situations, then analyze what occurred. Provide running commentary on the people you meet, the clients you serve, the environment in which you work, and the projects you are assigned. The journal is a safe place to confide your doubts, fears, hopes, and career aspirations. For best results, write regularly and be sure to include the date and time of each entry.

Case in Point

Tuesday, September 5
10:00 A.M.–12:00 P.M.

I had car trouble on the way to my internship today and arrived an hour late. I did remember to call, though, so nobody seemed upset with me. I volunteered to stay later tomorrow to make up the time. My supervisor seemed surprised that I was so dedicated.

The other intern doesn't seem to be doing her fair share when it comes to telephoning new members. I see her visiting with the secretaries when she is supposed to be making calls, and she leaves most of the work to me. I don't like making cold calls either and I don't want to be the only intern doing it.

I wonder if I should complain to my supervisor? Would that make me look disloyal to my peer? Would it make me look like a whiner? I don't think I'd be very good in a supervisory role because I dislike confrontation.

Critical Incidents. Describe and evaluate memorable incidents you encounter during your internship. Critical incidents include events, situations, and observations that arouse strong emotional responses such as frustration, fascination, fright, sympathy, sadness, or anger. There are four key steps to writing about or discussing critical incidents:

1. Describe what happened in detail.
2. Discuss your emotional reaction to what you observed or experienced.
3. Critique the way the incident was handled.
4. Provide your own approach for dealing with a similar situation.

Case in
Point

On Tuesday morning, September 19, I overheard my supervisor, Ms. Angel, criticizing her secretary for revealing some confidential information about one of the teaching staff. Ms. Angel used a loud, belligerent tone of voice:

Ms. Angel: How could you tell Mrs. Sweeny about Mr. Rudolf's accident? You know we aren't supposed to give any personal information to the parents!

Joan: Mrs. Sweeny kept asking me why David wasn't in class last week. She was very upset because her son won't work for any other teacher. I just told her about David's accident because she was so insistent. I'm really sorry, but I didn't think it could do any harm.

Ms. Angel: You aren't paid to make those kinds of decisions. You are just paid to be a secretary. I'll have to take this matter up with the board. (Joan starts to cry.)

I sympathized with Joan because Ms. Angel was treating her in such a disrespectful way. I know we shouldn't give out personal information about teachers but there's no excuse for rudeness. I would have questioned Joan further about exactly what she said. I wouldn't bring the matter to the board unless I was convinced Joan's behavior had done some real damage.

Internship Seminar. An internship discussion group, workshop, or seminar, often held concurrently with the internship experience, provides an intensive means of reflection and learning. Facilitated by the internship coordinator or a faculty member, this class can offer interns valuable opportunities to share internship experiences and concerns. Feedback and support from other interns are essential ingredients in developing skills in communication, problem solving, and career development. In some internship programs, academic classes and seminars are required to ensure academic credit.

Career Development Assignments. Tasks that help you learn more about yourself and the world of work as well as prepare you for the job search process could be part of your internship seminar's syllabus, or assigned by a sponsoring professor. You may be asked to conduct an information interview with someone at your internship site or an individual in the community who holds a job that appeals to you. The perspective of working professionals will provide you with valuable insight into your field of interest. Sample questions:

- What is a typical day on the job like for you?

- What do you like best about your job? Least?

- How did you find this job?

- What is your educational background and training?

- What is a typical career path in your field?

- What position would you like to hold in five years?

- What advice do you have for someone who wants to have a position like yours?

Independent Study. Interns may be sponsored by individual instructors or advisors. Meetings with a professor, along with discussions of assigned readings or papers, provide time for feedback and reflection. Oral and written reports on the internship site's culture, mission, history, and clients, and the intern's role are sometimes required.

The downside of this method of reflection is that it's often difficult to schedule times to regularly process the ongoing events that occur during a semester-long internship. One or two meetings to receive assignments followed by brief discussions of the completed work may not be enough to help you identify your learning goals or support in-depth evaluation of outcomes.

Task Analysis Log. Another approach to reflecting on your internship activities is to keep a task analysis log. It is easy to become so overwhelmed with the forest of your activities that you don't fully appreciate the individual trees—skills you are acquiring. By keeping track of and reflecting on your internship tasks and responsibilities in a formal way, you will find you are building a documentable repertoire of skills and accomplishments that will enhance your resume. Interns who keep a task analysis log are often surprised by the number of new skills they have developed. (See Example 7.)

Action Labels. Having a rich and descriptive vocabulary with which to comment on your internship experiences will help you tune in to the specific contributions you are making to the organization's mission and to the skills you are developing and honing. These action labels are not only useful in reflecting on

(Example 7)

Internship Task Analysis Log

Date	Task	Who Assigned	Where, When (Conditions)	How Long (Time)	Impact	Standards	Skills

your experiences, but they can also help you write a compelling summary of your internship on your resume as well as articulate relevant highlights at future job interviews. (See Example 8.)

(Example 8)

Action Labels

Advising
giving financial counsel, working in an educational system

Appraising
evaluating programs or services, judging property value

Assembling
putting together technical apparatus or equipment, collecting information into a coherent whole

Budgeting
outlining project costs, assuring money will not be spent in excess of funds

Calculating
performing mathematical computations

Coaching
guiding activities of an athletic team, tutoring

Collecting
obtaining money or services

Compiling
gathering numerical, statistical, or factual data

Coordinating
arranging events, information, activities in several locations

Corresponding
answering inquiries or soliciting business by mail, initiating letters to others

Counseling

helping people with personal or emotional concerns, family matters, life development concerns, careers, or financial problems

Creating

generating new ideas, devising new ways of problem solving, creating artistically

Dealing with Pressure

handling time pressure, deadlines, complaints, abuse from others

Designing

creating physical interiors of rooms, exteriors of buildings, programs, schemes

Desktop Publishing

creating public displays, brochures, flyers, newsletters

Developing Mathematical Models

devising models for scientific, behavioral, economic phenomena

Disciplining

controlling crowd behavior, children

Dispensing

distributing information to the public, materials, equipment, medicine

Displaying

showcasing ideas in artistic form, pictures for public display, products in store windows

Editing

correcting newspaper, magazine articles, book manuscripts

Entertaining

giving parties, social events, performing

Evaluating

assessing a program, judging performance

Examining

administering tests, making financial assessments, looking for symptoms

Fund-Raising

soliciting door-to-door, by mail, through advertising

Group Facilitating

managing interactions of groups, facilitating therapy

Handling Complaints
resolving problems for customers, stockholders, constituents, parents

Initiating
making personal contacts with strangers, devising new ideas, new approaches

Inspecting
evaluating physical objects to meet standards, people to determine criteria or detect information

Interpreting
translating languages, obscure phrases or passages, statistical data

Listening
being attentive to groups or individuals

Managing
being responsible for the work of others or for processing information, guiding activities of a team, having responsibility for meeting objectives of an organization or department

Measuring
obtaining accurate scientific measurement

Mediating
being a peacemaker, acting as a liaison between competing interests

Meeting the Public
being a receptionist, giving tours, representing your agency, selling products, serving the public

Monitoring
following the progress of a person or project

Motivating
inspiring others to achieve physical performance or make psychological efforts

Negotiating
working out financial contracts, resolving conflicts between individuals or groups

Observing
evaluating physical phenomena, human behavior, small details in physical objects, small details in written materials, social or historical phenomena

Obtaining Information

gathering data from written sources, documents, from unwilling individuals

Operating or Programming

working with scientific equipment, mechanical devices, computers

Organizing

bringing people together for certain tasks, gathering information and arranging it in clear, interpretable form, arranging political activity

Politicking

anticipating future needs of a company or organization, generating financial support, attempting to influence policy

Predicting

forecasting physical phenomena, psychological or social events, economic trends

Promoting

advertising through written or visual media

Protecting

protecting property, nature, people

Questioning

obtaining legal evidence, interviewing, obtaining information

Record Keeping

recording numerical data, keeping a log of sequential information, creating and maintaining files, accurate financial records, and service records

Recording

keeping numerical or quantitative data, scientific data, inputting data into computers

Recruiting

acquiring services of new employees

Researching

extracting information from library or archives, conducting surveys, obtaining information from physical data

Selling

marketing ideas through writing or speaking, selling products to individuals, policies to the public

Serving

providing service to an individual, serving a product such as food

Setting up

arranging for a demonstration of apparatus, getting people and things ready for a show, exhibit, or fair

Sketching

drawing pictures of things, people, producing charts, diagrams

Speaking

speaking publicly to an audience, to a group, through electronic media

Supervising

being directly responsible for the work of others

Teaching or Training

lecturing in school classrooms, teaching individuals to perform tasks, tutoring individuals, training new employees

Troubleshooting

finding sources of difficulty in human relations, detecting sources of difficulty in physical apparatus

Updating

keeping a file of information up-to-date, completing historical record of a person, acquiring new information on an old topic

Working in Laboratories

setting up scientific equipment, obtaining results from experiments

Working on Committees

creating and attaining objectives through committees

Working Outdoors

working with the land and its resources, with animals, testing oneself against physical challenges

Writing

copywriting for sales or advertising, creative writing, expository writing, proposal writing, technical writing

(Adapted from *Path, A Career Workbook for Liberal Arts Students*, Howard E. Figler, The Carroll Press, Cranston, RI, pp. 73–77.)

Portfolio. Portfolios documenting artistic or literary skills are commonly used by people seeking jobs in the arts. Comprising representative samples of related work, portfolios provide firsthand proof of skills and abilities. Interns can also document their skills by maintaining a tangible record of their internship contributions. Brochures, articles, flyers, invitations, programs, reports, newsletters, advertisements, photographs, company literature, computer printouts, customer contact lists, and letters provide documentation of relevant accomplishments.

Protect this information with plastic page protectors—labelled, ordered by time or theme—inserted into a simple multi-ring binder or more elaborate leather-bound, zippered portfolio case. Occasionally, confidentiality issues will prohibit your retaining sensitive materials. Before making copies of any of your work, check with your supervisor. In most cases, eliminating names from documents will ensure confidentiality so you can share materials with prospective employers. The old saying that "a picture is worth a thousand words" is definitely true when it comes to communicating your skills and abilities to others. A well-designed portfolio permits you to illustrate the points you want to make by referring to a display of your work. Portfolios are also a great way to organize your internship memories so that you can revisit them in the years to come.

"Try to **be** one of

those people on whom

nothing is lost."

Henry James

Right from the Start

Your Internship Experience

Getting Started

It isn't easy being the new kid on the block. It's even harder being the temporary new kid on the block, the kid who will move away in a few short months. A feeling of disorientation is typical the first few weeks as you learn where the file room is located, how lunch break protocol works, and what a typical day on the job is like. If you are fortunate enough to have a good supervisor, you will be taken on a tour of the facility and introduced to all the employees. Of course, you won't remember all the details or names right away, but an overview of the operation should put you on the right track. Speed the acclimatization process by requesting an organizational chart and filling in all the names and corresponding workstations.

This is the time to ask plenty of questions. Write them down as they occur to you and use these first weeks to collect as much information as possible about your internship responsibilities and how your role fits with organizational goals. Direct your questions to other workers and interns as well as to your supervisor. People usually like talking about their jobs and will give you interesting perspectives and information about all aspects of the organization. So the interaction doesn't feel like an interrogation, vary your questioning style from the traditional who, what, where, when, and why to phrases, such as: "I'm interested in knowing . . ." "I'd like to hear more about . . ." or "I don't think I know what you mean by . . . ."

When you are given oral instructions, try to paraphrase or summarize what is said to determine whether you have fully understood what you are supposed to do. For example: "You would like me to type this memo, give it to Mrs. Jones to check, correct it, make twenty copies, and stuff them in the prepared envelopes. Is that right?" Carry a notepad to help you remember your assignments or any helpful bits of relevant information.

Maintain a friendly, pleasant demeanor. Smile a lot and try to give no outward trace of tension, stress, or frustration. (Easier said than done.) Some employees will go out of their way to befriend you and make you feel welcome and needed; others may ignore you, feeling that investing their energies in a temporary intern isn't worth their time. Make an effort to talk to everyone at all points along the power hierarchy. Valuable information can be shared by the clerk typist and the night custodian as well as the president of the board of directors.

Fitting In

Employers frequently complain about their interns' unexplained absences, poor punctuality, and lack of professionalism. To avoid these problems, do your best to stick to the schedule you and your supervisor have agreed upon. If an emergency arises or you come down with the flu, call your supervisor. If you can't call, have your roommate do it for you. Be on time, even if it seems as if no one is keeping tabs on you. As a student, you often have the option of missing class and juggling your schedule to suit your needs. In the workplace, however, you need to follow a set work schedule because others depend on your contribution. Give your supervisor advance warning about your exam schedule, religious holidays, and other important events in your life that will necessitate time off or a readjustment of your schedule.

Join in the lunch or social activities of the group, even if you aren't issued a formal invitation. Remaining aloof will prevent you from getting the lowdown on the culture of the organization. Try not to segregate yourself by age. Since you're used to sharing lunchtime with peers, you may find it intimidating at first to make lunchtime chitchat with older employees and authority figures. Unlike the academic world, the working world is not segregated by age. Just jump right into the conversation: "How was your weekend?" "I heard you were out sick yesterday; are you feeling better today?" "Did you run into traffic problems on the way to work this morning?" "Is that your daughter's wedding picture on your desk?"

Look for topics in common but avoid emotionally charged topics such as politics, sex, or religion. Don't react to complaints about the organization and by no means offer complaints or criticism of your own. Pack your usual shyness with strangers away in mothballs but maintain some distance between yourself and the permanent staff, no matter how much you like them. Use your best judgment about socializing after working hours, and remember that your behavior will be scrutinized and evaluated no matter how friendly and informal your coworkers appear to be on the surface.

Follow the organizational dress code. Men should avoid earrings and both men and women should avoid earrings in places other than earlobes unless there is a clear message that this alternative style is acceptable. Casual dress may be tolerated, but in general, more respect is given to interns who look the part of a professional. Dress for the role you would like to play in the organization if you were offered a full-time position after graduation. If you are invited to a social occasion outside work that calls for informal dress, be sure your clothing is somewhat conservative. Remind yourself that judgments about your professionalism are also made after hours.

Understanding Your Internship Role

Try to keep high expectations in check. Your first internship tasks may be on the order of grunt or gofer work, unchallenging jobs you would prefer to avoid, such as copying and filing or carrying materials from one office to another. Even though these tasks don't appear on the surface to meet your learning goals, remember that the early days are a time when your supervisor and coworkers may be sizing you up for bigger and more challenging responsibilities. Your positive attitude toward pitching in and doing what needs to be done will not go unnoticed or unappreciated. When undertaken with the right spirit, even the most mundane tasks can often offer you a unique opportunity to learn more about your organization.

Don't immediately attempt to impress everyone with what you know. Volunteer your thoughts and views but don't try to dazzle everyone with your innovative ideas right away. It is expected that the new kid will spend some time learning the ropes and figuring out the organizational culture before attempting to make a mark. Your friendliness, patience, and willingness to learn on the job will be your most helpful attributes in the early weeks and months.

Curiosity and an inquiring attitude will do wonders to help you bypass or move quickly through the second predictable internship stage—*Disillusionment*. Many interns report that by the end of the third week of their internship, they have moved from the excitement of the *Anticipation Stage* to the frustration of the *Disillusionment Stage* (Sweitzer and King). Interns need to confront the gap between their high expectations and the realities of their internship through effective communication with their supervisors.

Using a Winning Approach

As a new intern, what strategies will help you deal successfully with such typical start-up frustrations as tedious, routine assignments and lack of structure? In a nutshell, you need to keep your eyes peeled, your ears open, and your mind engaged so you can fully understand and appreciate the organizational meaning and implications of everything you observe and everything you do.

Read all the correspondence and memos you type or copy. The same goes for bills, meeting minutes, brochures, faxes, forms, budgets—any written communication or printed material passing through your hands. Don't file anything without reading it first. Ask yourself: What value does this item have for this organization? How will it be used? Who would be doing my job if I weren't available? You can learn a great deal about the inner workings of an organization—its priorities and problems—by reading everything you can. Not enough to do? Spend some time reading a copy of your organization's annual report or minutes from the last board of directors' meeting. Become an expert on your internship site's history.

Answering the telephone? By listening carefully, you can learn a lot about clients or customers who interact regularly with your internship site. Pay attention to the talk around you. You can pick up a lot of valuable information about office politics and culture this way. Do the employees seem to be pulling together as a team? Is there open dissension? How are the secretaries treated? Is everyone on a first-name basis? Are there some people who seem to be scapegoats? Even office gossip and personal chatter over lunch can furnish clues about the overall organization. Be careful, though, not to offer criticism or negative comments about any aspect of your internship. Negativity in newcomers is rarely tolerated and could come back to haunt you.

Carefully observe your physical surroundings. How are space and resources allocated? What is your workspace like? What does the office decor say about the organization's funding and priorities? Be prepared to describe and comment on the working conditions that exist in your internship organization.

Ask if you can attend staff meetings, conferences, and lectures to get further insight into the issues that regularly affect your internship organization. Go out on sales calls, observe seminars, sit in on professional association meetings. Find out about purchasing, inventory, budgeting, and the nuts and bolts of your organization. Try to get a sense of where your organization fits into the world of work.

In addition to your supervisor, other workers can serve as role models, sources of information, and contacts in your field. Occasionally, full-time employees exhibit some negativity toward interns because they envy their flexible schedules or resent having to spend time training novices who won't be around long enough to apply their newly acquired skills. More often than not, however, your colleagues will be eager to take you under their wings, appreciate your help, and get a charge out of your enthusiasm for tasks that they may consider old hat. Watch your coworkers carefully, paying attention to those activities that consume the bulk of their time. Do some informal information interviewing, questioning them about their career development in the field as well as future career plans.

Dealing with Your Supervisor

13

Internship supervisors run the gamut from attentive, involved, and reinforcing to distant—both physically and emotionally. This is true for any workplace. Some supervisors take on the role of mentor, carefully structuring relevant activities and offering ongoing advice to help you meet your learning goals. Consistent feedback on your progress, compliments, and constructive criticism characterize this supervisory style.

On the other hand, your supervisor may leave the monitoring of your activities and behavior to others, appear distracted by other concerns, and sometimes leave you in the lurch, not knowing what you should do next or whether your work products are acceptable. Some supervisors will respect your time constraints as a student; others frequently ask you to put in extra time, creating conflicts among academic, personal, and internship schedules.

Students concur that the best internship supervisors exhibit the following traits:

■ approachable

■ interested in your academic and career goals

■ give assignments that balance grunt work with more substantive tasks

■ monitor your activities through regular meetings

■ provide feedback   .

■ help you meet your goals as stated in your learning contract

■ provide adequate resources, materials, and money to allow you to complete your assigned tasks

■ show appreciation for what you do

■ give you advice about your career path

■ try to integrate you with the regular staff

■ view your mistakes as learning opportunities

■ introduce you to others who can help with your career

- give you the chance to learn new skills

- allow you to take part in projects where you can be involved from beginning to end

- provide you with a reference for your credential file or dossier

Whatever your supervisor's style or traits, try to communicate with him or her on a regular basis. It's natural to experience some unease during your initial interactions with your supervisor; after all, you are dealing with your boss. The attainment of your learning goals and the ultimate success of your internship, however, depend in large measure on maintaining open lines of communication with your supervisor.

After an initial honeymoon period, the time may come when you need to confront your supervisor or coworkers about incongruencies between your expectations and the realities you face. Your supervisor or coworkers may also have occasion to confront you about your performance on the job. *Confrontation*, a necessary and predictable stage that follows the excitement of the *Anticipation Stage* and the anxiety of the *Disillusionment Stage*, entails actively addressing and resolving problems as they occur, rather than brooding about them or complaining to others (Sweitzer and King). Confrontation, when handled appropriately, increases your chances of resolving sticky wickets so you can move smoothly into the *Competency Stage* where you should experience a heightened sense of self-confidence and efficacy.

Communicating with Your Supervisor

Most interns can benefit from learning communication techniques to initiate, address, and react to sensitive subjects. Mastering a tried-and-true formula for assertive communication will ease your way. This is not to say all your questions, statements, and answers must mimic this formula; your natural language is best. When dealing with a sensitive subject, remember to:

■ Start with a positive statement or point of agreement.

■ Be specific about what you would prefer to have happen; suggest alternatives.

■ Provide a brief rationale or explanation.

■ Check out your supervisor's or coworker's reactions.

■ Express your thanks for the time and attention others have given to your issue.

The following scenarios provide guidelines to encourage you to speak to your supervisor in an effective, nonoffensive way about issues that may affect your ability to meet your internship goals.

Asking for Feedback

Case in Point

Jed has been working at the Tormee law firm for three weeks but has no idea if his performance is acceptable to his supervisor. "I think I'm doing a good job," he says to his fellow intern, "but except for showing me some documents, my supervisor hasn't said a word to me."

TIP

Feedback in the workplace tends to be more sporadic than in the classroom where assignments are usually graded in a timely fashion. It will often be up to you to initiate discussion with your supervisor about your performance.

Jed might say to his internship supervisor: "I've really been learning a lot from the assignments you have given me but I'm not sure if I am approaching them the best way. I'd really like to get some feedback from you about my work on the Marcus and Doming cases. When could we set up some time to discuss this?" After receiving a positive response, Jed should express his appreciation: "Thanks a lot. I think your comments will help."

Asking for More or Different Assignments

Case in Point

Martha wants to learn all she can about the role of a stockbroker in an investment firm. For the past month, however, her supervisor has given her only basic clerical tasks that she mastered on the second day. "How will I know if I want to be a stockbroker if I never get any hands-on experience," she grumbles to her roommate. "I chose this internship because I was told I would have the chance to do a lot of different things."

TIP

You can expect a certain amount of grunt work to be part of any internship. Paying attention to all assigned tasks, no matter how mundane, and reflecting on the meaning these tasks have for the organization is instructive, for a while at least. After several weeks have elapsed, however, it is probably time to talk to your supervisor about adding more challenging work that will help you meet your internship goals.

Martha could say to her supervisor: "The assignments you have given me so far have really taught me a lot about the daily operations of a brokerage firm. Now I'm hoping to branch out and try some new things. Bob offered to train me on Lotus and I'd really like to attend some of the Friday investment conferences. Would this be possible?" After her supervisor's response, Martha should express her appreciation: "Thank you very much."

Turning Down a Request

Case in Point

Ms. Davidson calls her intern, Lisa, aside to beg her to come to an emergency session on a Saturday morning to stuff envelopes for the fund-raising campaign. "Everyone on the staff will be there and we'll work all day until the job is done." Lisa has already made plans to travel 200 miles to visit her aunt.

TIP

Interns need to maintain flexibility and show they are willing to take on their share of the organization's mission, above and beyond their normal hours if necessary. But there are times when they feel torn between a desire to show they are part of the team, willing to pitch in like everybody else, and the need to honor prior commitments.

Lisa could say to her internship supervisor: "I know how important this campaign is to the Salvation March but I won't be able to help on Saturday because I am going out of town. I'm really sorry. Could I work some extra hours this week or next to help out?"

Asking for Clarification or Help

Case in Point

Wynn's supervisor assigned her a project that not only seemed vague and confusing but also required a higher level of skill with computers than she had.

TIP

It's difficult to confess to a supervisor that you need additional help, but it is important not to fake an understanding that you simply don't have.

Wynn could say to her supervisor: "This project sounds really interesting and I want to help, but I need to get more information on how to find all the names and addresses for the donors and how to enter the data into the computer. Can you set some time aside to work with me or is there someone else who could help me?"

Ensuring Absent Supervisors Leave You Assignments

Case in Point

During the third week of her internship, Jackie arrived at her site to find that her supervisor was absent and hadn't told anyone what she was supposed to do. Jackie felt foolish as she sat at her desk for two hours doing nothing.

TIP

It is very frustrating for an intern to go to work only to find that his or her supervisor is gone and no one knows what he or she should do. Sometimes you have an ongoing project you can work on. Other times you can ask coworkers if they have something for you to do. If you are left with no structured assignments, read company literature to learn more about the company, conduct information interviews with your coworkers, or write in your internship journal.

When her supervisor returns, Jackie could say: "When you aren't here, I'm not sure what activities you want me to get going on. It would really help if you could leave a list of things you want me to do when you have to be away."

Receiving Negative Feedback

Case in Point

Blake addressed postcards to the chief financial officers of forty organizations rather than to the human resources managers. Her supervisor brought this mistake to her attention.

TIP

Even the most diligent intern will occasionally misstep or ruffle some feathers and can expect to receive some constructive criticism. It is important to take this feedback calmly, without going on the defensive. Supervisors know it is impossible to learn without making some mistakes. It's seldom the end of the world. Make sure you apologize and think of a way that you can correct the mistake. Assure your supervisor you will do your best not to make the same mistake again.

Blake could say to her supervisor: "I must have copied the first name on the list rather than the second. I'm really sorry. How can I correct the error? Should I address new postcards to the right people, or should I call the human resources managers to let them know about the upcoming meeting? I will double-check the lists in the future when there are two names mentioned. This won't happen again."

Handling an Unobserved Error

Case in Point

While his supervisor was away, Marc upset one of the bedridden patients at the Harvest Nursing Home by mentioning he had taken another patient, who was more mobile, out for a walk. The nurses had to increase the patient's medication to calm her agitation because she demanded to have a walk, too. Marc realized that he shouldn't have talked about one patient's activities to another.

T I P

> If you are aware that you did something wrong or were responsible for a problem situation, go immediately to your supervisor to tell him or her about it. Do not let your supervisor hear about it from other people. Don't ask others to keep silent about your error. Honesty is definitely the best policy in all situations.

Marc could say to his supervisor: "Yesterday, I made the mistake of discussing Mrs. Ackerman's outdoor exercise with Mrs. DeRies. She got very upset because I couldn't take her outside for exercise, too, and the nurses had to medicate her. I feel really bad about this and now realize I have to be very careful about what I say to one patient about another. I won't make this mistake again."

Solving Other Problem Situations

You find your workspace is inadequate to get your assignments done. Someone else is using your space when you aren't there and you can't find your projects when you return. Come up with a script to address this problem with your supervisor.

_____

_____

_____

_____

_____

One of the regular employees has made a mistake in proofreading the brochure you designed and claims you are responsible for the errors. It's his word against yours. What do you say to your supervisor?

_____

_____

_____

_____

_____

Your internship just isn't working out and you decide to leave. How do you explain this to your supervisor?

_____

_____

_____

_____

_____

Encounters
with
Coworkers

Dealing with your coworkers on the job calls for tact and diplomacy. No matter how comfortable you become in your internship, maintain some professional distance between you and your temporary colleagues.

The following scenarios offer advice for dealing effectively with your coworkers.

Reacting to Criticism of Others

Case in Point

Jenna was having some tea in the lounge when she heard two of the staff talking about Ms. Campbell, her supervisor. "I can't believe how cheap she is; after all my overtime and extra projects, I didn't even get a decent raise," complained one person. "If you ask me, she's hiding this year's profits under her pillow," replied the other. They both turned to Jenna to hear what she had to say on the subject.

T I P

Criticizing your supervisor, coworkers, or fellow interns is a bad move. As a student, griping about poor professors and insensitive administrators is a commonly accepted practice and doesn't usually have any serious consequences. Any negative comments you make in the workplace, however, have a good chance of reaching the subject's ears and poisoning relationships. On the other hand, saying nothing at all or vociferously defending your supervisor or an unpopular colleague may serve to alienate your coworkers.

In her response, Jenna could focus on the unvoiced feelings behind the angry words being expressed by saying: "It's hard to stay motivated when you don't feel appreciated." By responding in this way, she has supported her coworkers without denigrating her supervisor.

Overhearing an Argument Between Coworkers

Case in Point

Ryan was busy stuffing envelopes and typing memos at his desk when he heard two of the other workers in the room beginning to argue. "I could have handled that telephone call without your help, Marge. Why do you always feel you have to take every call?" "I have to jump in because you don't really know what you're doing, George." Their voices rose until they were shouting. Ryan was beginning to feel very uncomfortable.

T I P

It is inevitable that tempers will sometimes flare in the workplace. If you hear an angry exchange like this one, leave the room, if possible, before you are privy to any more heated words. If you remain on the scene, you run the risk that, long after the argument has been resolved, the participants will be embarrassed because you witnessed their lack of professionalism.

Ryan's best bet is to say nothing and leave the room.

Declining Personal Invitations

Case in Point

Jeri's internship at the chamber of commerce is just about perfect except for the unwelcome attentions of Steve, one of the younger staff members. On several occasions, Steve has asked Jeri to go out for a drink after work, have lunch with him, or go to a movie on the weekend. Jeri has politely declined each invitation, but Steve just can't seem to take the hint that she is not interested in a personal relationship. Jeri is beginning to feel apprehensive about coming to work because she doesn't want to face Steve.

T I P

It's probably a good idea to avoid after-hours relationships with individual coworkers of the opposite sex, at least until your internship ends.

Steve's overtures are coming dangerously close to sexual harassment, since his repeated invitations are unwelcome and are causing Jeri to experience discomfort on the job. There are several actions she can take to address this situation:

1. Write a note or speak to Steve and say firmly: "Thank you for the invitation, Steve, but I don't want to mix my personal and professional life. Please don't ask me out again because I'll just keep saying 'no.'"

2. Speak to her supervisor about the situation and ask for help in dealing with it.
3. Speak to the organization's Equal Employment Opportunity Officer or a personnel official.
4. Discuss this matter with her school's internship faculty sponsor or career services office.

Voicing Negative Comments About Internship Activities

Case in Point

It seemed to Jordan that all he did during his internship was type labels and mail out flyers. One day he grumbled out loud to one of the secretaries: "I can't believe they have me doing such mindless work. You don't even need a high school education to do what I am doing." Later, he wondered why the secretaries were cool toward him.

TIP

While grunt or gofer work is the least enriching of your internship activities, you should keep your frustrations to yourself. For many secretaries, the work you disdain is an important part of their job description. When you demean the work they do, it may appear you are demeaning them. Be sensitive to the feelings of workers at all levels of the organizational hierarchy.

Jordan could say to the secretary he offended: "I'm sorry I was griping about the mailing yesterday. I hope what I said didn't bother you. I know this work must be done and I'll try to be in a better mood in the future." Jordan's best tactic when encountering a similar situation in the future is to address his concerns directly to his supervisor or suffer in silence.

Solving Other Problem Situations

Maggie, one of the younger employees, often shares information about her personal life such as fights with her boyfriend or holiday plans and seems eager to have you do the same. Use the space below to write a script of your possible reaction.

_____

_____

_____

_____

_____

_____

Most of your fellow interns and workers are parents. You have noticed that at break time they talk nonstop about their children. You feel a bit out of it. What could you do to increase the rapport with your colleagues?

_____

_____

_____

_____

_____

_____

_____

How's Your Internship Shaping Up?

It's several weeks into your internship. You've been oriented to the organization, have a good idea about what's expected of you, and are on your way to building good relationships with your supervisor and colleagues. By now you are probably beginning to discern a definite pattern of assigned tasks taking shape, a pattern that will fit one of five common internship tracks: *Observer, Odd Jobs, Prime Function, Project Centered,* or *Apprentice.* Chances are, your internship track wasn't described to you at the time of your interview. Your prospective supervisor may not have known at that point what the actual trajectory of your internship would be. Regardless of the particular internship track you find yourself on, however, each path has the potential to assist you in meeting your goals by providing career information, networking opportunities, skill development, and valuable experience. Becoming attuned early on to the shape of your internship will help you maximize its unique possibilities or work to make appropriate adjustments.

The Observer Track. As its name suggests, the *Observer Track* emphasizes watching and assessing rather than hands-on participation. *Observer Tracks* show up most often for short-term experiences when there isn't enough time to involve the intern too intimately with the organization's activities. Students have the chance to observe professionals in action, to ask questions about the workplace, and to read background material. There is a similarity between this internship model and shadowing programs, short-term experiences where students follow or shadow the activities of workers in occupations of interest.

The *Observer Track* comes into play when confidentiality issues or lack of professional training prohibit students from full participation in an internship site's daily operations. If your internship model fits the *Observer Track*, you will have the chance to gain a broad-brush look at a worksite. With close attention and reflection, you should be able to gather valuable information about your field of interest and the daily activities of employees.

Case in

Point

Jessica arranged for an internship in the human resources department of a large university to learn more about how it functioned. Each week for fourteen weeks her supervisor set up meetings for her to attend: new employee orientations, advisory board councils, labor relations seminars. Information interviews were arranged for her with affirmative action officers, the women's center coordinator, minority affairs officials, and training personnel. She was exposed to employee services she had known nothing about, such as career development workshops, fitness programs, and employee assistance programs. Jessica was enthused about how much she was learning in this well-structured environment, which she characterized as a series of mini-classrooms and lectures.

Since Jessica was introduced to so many individuals and was shuffled through so many departments, names and faces became a blur. So Jessica made it a point to collect business cards from each person she met so she could arrange follow-up meetings with those employees whose jobs were of particular interest to her or who could become part of her network. After her extensive introduction, Jessica decided she wanted to do another internship in human resources, one that would focus in-depth on one facet of the field. Jessica summarized the good points of her internship: "I got a lot of my questions answered about the field of human resources and I also learned listening and questioning skills that can draw people out to get the information I'm looking for."

Case in Point

Dan was a criminal justice major whose goal was to go to law school following graduation. Since he had a five-week break between the fall and spring semesters, he applied for a short-term internship at the state attorney general's office. On the first day of his internship, Dan's supervisor, the attorney general's administrative aide, showed him into a small room and told him to read the files of two pending cases. The next day, he was taken to the courtroom to view the two cases in progress. This set the pattern for his internship. In the morning, he would read a case and later, observe trials. Every Friday, Dan had a regularly scheduled fifteen-minute appointment with the attorney general to ask questions about the proceedings.

Dan was given the chance to observe a variety of cases dealing with everything from custody to assault and murder. The administrative aide structured the internship so that Dan was always busy either reading about cases, viewing the court proceedings, or meeting with the attorney general. "I really saw the

T I P

If your internship fits the *Observer Track*, you will gain exposure to various facets of your field of interest plus have the chance to make contacts to add to your network. This type internship is very helpful in identifying specific areas that warrant more thorough investigation in the future. The *Observer Track* encourages the development and application of listening skills, questioning techniques, and the ability to interact with many people. Inevitably, you will be able to make connections between textbook knowlege and real-world settings. A participant in the *Observer Track* has to make a concerted effort to overcome potential feelings of detachment or isolation by pursuing relationships with employees at the worksite.

legal profession come to life during those five weeks,"
wrote Dan in his journal. "It was scary to see what a
difficult job lawyers have. I may rethink my decision
to go to law school."

The Odd Jobs Track. Because so many organizations
today are short-staffed and overworked, managers
often view internship programs primarily as a cost-
effective means of adding staff while, incidentally, giving students the benefit of exposure to their field of
choice. The resulting internship can sometimes be a
patchwork of tasks that are assigned to interns because
regular employees don't have the time or energy to do
them. In this situation, interns are shifted from one
task to another without a coherent plan or explanation. While many of these tasks may be of consider-
able interest, it's often difficult for interns to see how
each job fits into the big picture. Without an obvious
structure or context, many tasks can seem pointless
and unchallenging.

If you find yourself on the *Odd Jobs Track*, you need
to be especially proactive in asking questions, locat-
ing background information, and initiating projects
that will help you meet your internship goals. Enlist
the support of your supervisor in devising ways to
help the overwhelmed staff while still providing
opportunities for you to learn how the organization
functions and spend some time on projects that will
best serve your interests.

Case in

Point

The staff at Barnett & Hobbs, Inc., a stockbrokerage firm, warmly welcomed their new intern, Chris, on the first day of his internship. Since their administrative assistant had left weeks before, the staff was hard-pressed to complete all their work in a timely manner. They hoped Chris could take up some of the slack while getting experience in the field. After a brief tour of the building, his supervisor called out: "Who needs help today?" Chris was then assigned to work with the employee who had asked the loudest.

This pattern held true for the first month of his internship. Chris was always coming in on the middle of some activity in progress—checking figures against a computer printout, reserving rooms at a local hotel for a financial planning meeting, typing labels for folders, inputting client data into the computer, or calling clients to see if they had received special materials. Chris enjoyed most of the tasks and liked his colleagues, but he had trouble forming more than a jumbled impression of how a brokerage firm operates. Because his internship hours were so crammed with disjointed assignments, Chris had to take the initiative to make some changes, coming in before normal hours to discuss the business with his supervisor. To better understand the big picture, Chris requested company literature and set up a field trip to corporate headquarters.

"I had to go the extra mile to get a full picture of how things worked at Barnett & Hobbs," Chris wrote in his journal, "because nothing was hanging together for me. They treated me like a temporary worker who was just there to help out in a crunch. I was glad to do whatever they needed but I also wanted to understand how everything fit together. As long as I did my assignments, my supervisor was glad to give me all the information and advice I wanted."

T I P

The *Odd Jobs Track* offers you a smorgasbord of experience in your field of interest and numerous contacts with a usually appreciative staff. You will have the chance to experience at least some of the tasks that are an integral part of your field and develop new skills. The downside is that you may not be able to get involved with projects from start to finish or see the outcome of your particular contribution. Additionally, your time could well be monopolized by random tasks that are not fully explained or provided a context.

In order to get the most out of this type of internship, it is vital to seize the day, enlisting the help of
your coworkers and supervisor in building your
understanding of the organization. Take the initiative
and suggest projects and activities you can pursue
from beginning to end. Ask to attend meetings, read
company literature, and think of interesting questions
to research.

Prime Function Track. Some internships expose students intensively to only one primary task or set of
tasks. Students gain increasing competence in one facet
of an organization, thoroughly learning the correct
practices and procedures to the point where they often
perform their jobs independent of supervision. In the
Prime Function Track student interns are seen as vital
contributors to the important mission of the organization and are usually provided with careful orientations, attentive supervision, helpful feedback, and
requests for input. If you have an internship like this,
you will have a high degree of autonomy as your
coworkers develop confidence in your growing capa-
bilities. On the other hand, the fly in the ointment is
that you have to stick with these primary tasks with
little or no opportunity to vary your assignments or
participate in other aspects of the organization.
Attempts to broaden your internship tasks may be met
with resistance because coworkers have come to
depend on your contribution to the organization.

Case in Point

Since Suzanne had a deep interest in women's issues, she was very excited to see that a local nonprofit agency, which operated a battered women's shelter, was looking for an intern. During her interview at the shelter, Suzanne was given a tour of the whole operation. She was shown the counseling rooms, the living quarters, the kitchen, and the sunny room where children of the residents could watch TV or play games. All of the aspects of the shelter were explained to her in detail and she couldn't wait to get started. After a week of orientation, Suzanne was assigned to the playroom to care for the children. Suzanne took to her new job like a duck to water. It became immediately clear to her supervisor and coworkers that Suzanne was a natural born teacher who had an affinity for children of all ages. She became adept at toning down the more boisterous children and bringing the quieter ones out of their shells. She devised games, put on puppet shows, and designed arts and crafts projects. The regular staff, as well as the residents, let Suzanne know what an excellent job she was doing.

After several weeks, however, Suzanne asked her supervisor if she could participate in some other functions of the shelter. "I really need you in the playroom, " her supervisor said. "In fact, if you have extra time, I'd like you to spend it all in the playroom. You do such a great job!" Suzanne was flattered by her supervisor's praise and was glad to help with the children, but she was frustrated by the fact that she wasn't going to be given the chance to learn more about administrative or counseling tasks. "I sort of boxed myself into working in the playroom and there didn't seem to be a way out," she said. "So I decided that after my internship was over I would volunteer some time in the shelter office so I could learn more about the budget, fund-raising, security, and other issues that interest me."

The *Prime Function Track* offers you the opportunity to develop and demonstrate competency in specific areas, often giving you professional levels of responsibility and autonomy. Your supervisors and coworkers encourage your creativity and fresh ideas, value your work, and depend on your contribution. There is ample opportunity to build your skills and your self-confidence. Some interns, however, may feel pigeonholed and wish they could be exposed to the full range of organizational tasks and functions. If that's true for you, consider other internships or volunteer roles to experience the full complement of organizational activities.

The Project Track. Many organizations use interns for special projects that the regular staff do not have time to carry out. The intern is given the unique opportunity to see a project through from beginning to end, often requiring creativity, research skills, organizational abilities, and self-direction. With few guidelines, you may have lots of latitude in developing and carrying out a project that demands challenging and diverse skills. Like most interns, you will probably find this type of internship very rewarding because it gives you the chance to leave your own stamp on the organization. The chief drawbacks of the *Project Track* center around the potential lack of integration between the intern and the regular staff and the difficulty in getting a feel for the culture and daily activities of the organization as a whole.

Case in Point

Sharon was hired as an intern by the state department of health to develop a much-needed resource guide for senior citizens that could be distributed by hospitals, clinics, senior centers, and mental health facilities throughout the region. She was given a budget of $500, a small alcove off the administrator's office, and unlimited access to the telephone and computer. Sharon's supervisor, a public health nurse, explained that she was too busy to provide much, if any, support for the project. "You're on your own, Sharon," she said. "You told me in your internship interview that you were a self-starter and here's your chance to prove it."

Sharon's first step was to use the yellow pages and the city's directory of human resources to identify agencies that dealt with the elderly and their concerns. Next, she designed, printed, and mailed a survey of senior services to each agency on the list, following up with a phone call to those agencies that failed to respond to the initial mailing. After all the responses to the survey were tabulated, Sharon typed up one-page summaries of the services offered to senior citizens by each organization. After designing a cover and table of contents and adding illustrations, she used desktop publishing software to put together a booklet detailing information about the services for the elderly offered by more than sixty-five regional organizations. Then she shopped around to see which print shop could mass produce the booklet at the most reasonable cost. Finally, Sharon personally distributed five thousand copies of the *Senior Resource Guide* to each of the contributing organizations as well as to hospitals and public libraries.

It was very gratifying for Sharon to have full charge of this project from beginning to end and to actually see tangible results of her efforts. She received very positive comments and letters from social workers and health professionals throughout the nonprofit community and added many names to her personal network. Sharon made a point of introducing her booklet at subsequent job interviews to illustrate some of her strongest skills.

"I really got the chance to make a difference to the community," Sharon wrote in her journal. "The state department of health really needed the *Senior Resources Guide* but no one had the time to work on it until I came along. It was a fantastic experience all around and I think it will open some doors for me in the future."

The advantages of the *Project Track* internship tend to outweigh the disadvantage of isolation from other employees and the regular operation of your organization. Like Sharon, you relish having ownership of the project—making all the decisions from conception to distribution of the final product. Minimal input from your supervisor tends to allow free rein to use your organizational and communication skills to their fullest extent, complementing your independent work style. It's always a good idea, though, to keep your supervisor apprised of your daily accomplishments and progress toward your goal.

The Apprentice Track. Students recognize the *Apprentice Track* early on in their internships because they are clearly being treated like full-fledged, although junior, employees, rather than as temporary interns. After an initial orientation to office practices and procedures, they are expected to begin contributing their ideas, talents, and skills. Success with assigned tasks is rewarded by more complex assignments. Close super-vision gives way to increasing levels of independence and autonomy. Interns who rise to the challenge, catch on quickly, and demonstrate an aptitude for the work are groomed for full-time job openings.

Case in Point

After student teaching a junior high English class, Eric decided teaching English wasn't for him. Not knowing what else was available for an English major, he turned to his career center to find an internship that might help him identify a new career direction. An internship opportunity at Parker Associates, Inc., a small advertising agency, caught his attention and he decided to apply. Though he didn't know much about advertising, Eric was hired as an intern because of his enthusiasm about the position.

Right from the start, Eric was treated as an inex-perienced, but integral, part of the team. He was given the same tools, equipment, and workspace as the actual copywriters and was expected to take part in all tasks from writing press releases to brainstorming campaign ideas to attending client meetings. One of the regular workers would explain how to write a press release or devise a marketing plan, and Eric was expected to produce. Within a few days, his news releases began to appear in the local paper and his public service announcements were heard on radio. When the company's vice president discovered Eric's computer skills, he asked for a demonstration on how to set up a home page for Parker Associates, Inc., on the Internet. Eventually, one of Eric's marketing ideas was adopted and used in an advertising campaign for one of Parker's biggest clients. In a short time, he began to build a portfolio of his reports, press releases, ads, and other copy to show visual proof of his new skills. Toward the end of his internship, Eric was offered a full-time position with Parker Associates following his graduation from college. "This internship helped me get my feet wet in a new field. I'll probably take the job at Parker for a couple of years to get more experience," Eric wrote.

The *Apprentice Track* offers you the chance to prove yourself in an environment where expectations are high and challenges numerous. There is little time to play the role of a novice. If you adapt quickly and master the requisite skills, there is plenty of opportunity to enter into the fray and begin to actively contribute to your organization's mission. Your daily behavior and work products provide a sample of your performance that can go a long way toward persuading your supervisor to hire you or recommend you for another full-time position in the field.

What track does your present or past internship follow? Explain your reasoning.

_____

_____

_____

_____

_____

_____

_____

_____

The Competence Stage

"**W**e're opening a new office across town next week," Anna announced in her internship seminar. "Clients from other parts of the city will finally have access to our services, too." Anna's use of the words "we" and "our" is typical of interns who have reached the *Competence Stage* of their internships (Sweitzer and King). Having negotiated the *Anticipation, Disillusionment,* and *Confrontation* stages, seasoned interns find themselves identifying with their organization's mission and feeling a heightened sense of commitment. Morale is definitely at its peak.

You know when you have hit this stage because your self-confidence and self-esteem are on the rise.

You are now familiar with your regular assignments and acclimated to the work environment, and as the result of positive feedback from colleagues and supervisors, you feel confident about the organizational value of your skills and contributions. This new sense of security is usually accompanied by an increase in autonomy and control over your time and priorities. For the most part, you act and react more like a full-time employee than a temporary intern. Relationships become more reciprocal as some coworkers solicit your opinions and advice and tend to treat you as a colleague. At this point, you may even begin to feel comfortable offering coworkers your take on the work at hand and asserting your position on important issues. In some cases, it may be the right time to approach your supervisor about adding further autonomy and challenge to your internship mix.

Unfortunately, your new professional status may make it more difficult to carry out your responsibilities as a student. Some interns begin to experience impatience and frustration with their school assignments. Term papers and midterm exams seem increasingly irrelevant in light of the real-life events taking place at your internship site. The respect for your ideas shown by colleagues may contrast starkly with the more dismissive or critical reactions of professors. Despite this tension, don't neglect the academic side of the equation. Whenever possible, try to to use examples drawn from your internship experience to make compelling points in your term papers or class discussions. Bear in mind that successful completion of your coursework is necessary to ensure your full-time participation in most jobs.

Some interns find that on the flip side of growing feelings of competence are insights about limitations and problems with the management, funding, and staffing of their internship organization. Many hours of close observation on the job can reveal the organization's feet of clay. All those hours of study and observation help you spot examples of poor performance or lack of professionalism in the way business is conducted.

"There's so much visiting and small talk during working hours that it interferes with getting the job done, but no one in charge seems to notice or care," observed one intern halfway through her internship. Another student, interning at a health care agency, was distressed when she witnessed the staff discussing the need for more community nutrition programs while drinking soda and snacking on potato chips and dip. "How could they sit there and talk about healthy diets when their own diets are filled with sugar, fat, and cholesterol?"

Because of the temporary nature of most internships, it is probably best to keep negative observations such as these to yourself, confine them to your journal, or share them with your school's internship coordinator or seminar leader. Since you are a visitor to the workplace, your unsolicited criticism will probably be viewed as inappropriate at best and rude or ungrateful at worst.

Another common reaction reported by interns who have reached the *Competence Stage* are feelings of betrayal when regular staff take some or all of the credit for the interns' achievements or fail to publicly acknowledge their contributions. "I am the one who put together the agency newsletter but this one guy who doesn't know anything about desktop publishing was getting all the praise," commented an intern during her academic seminar. If this happens to you, try to stay cool and calm. Get your rewards from oral and written expressions of appreciation and the inner satisfaction of doing work of such high caliber that a professional staff member has claimed it for his or her own.

Your successful passage through the *Competence Stage* will be influenced by your internship's particular trajectory. For example, of all the internship tracks, the *Observer Track* is least conducive to fostering reciprocal relationships between you and the staff. If you are moving around from office to office or observing various professionals perform their tasks, it is difficult to take on an active role in any one area. While proactive interns may take steps to further integrate themselves into their internship organization, resistance by supervisors and coworkers makes this a formidable task. As a result, most interns operating in the *Observer* paradigm tend to bypass the full-blown *Competence Stage*. Nevertheless, the path your internship takes shouldn't be used as an excuse for failing to meet many or all of your internship goals.

Exiting
Your
Internship

The final weeks of your internship can be as diffi-cult as your first weeks, but for different reasons. If your internship has been successful, by this time you have established yourself as an integral part of your organization with a respected role. Many of your coworkers have become mentors and friends. You have built significant relationships with clients or custom-ers. At long last you are seeing some tangible results of your hours of hard work. The conclusion of your internship means summing up the contributions you have made, saying your good–byes to many people who have come to mean a lot to you, and letting go of projects and duties over which you feel ownership.

It's no wonder that the final phase of your internship, the *Culmination Stage* (Sweitzer and King), is fraught with conflicting emotions.

In the last days of your internship, expect some type of formal evaluation from your supervisor. It could take the form of an exit interview, a written evaluation, or an oral discussion with you, your internship coordinator, or a faculty sponsor. The evaluation process offers you the opportunity to reflect on the internship as a whole as well as on your strengths, shortcomings, and contributions. While such meetings may make you uncomfortable, performance reviews will continue to be a necessary feature of any job in your future and are directly related to salary increases and promotions. Another topic of discussion may be your insights about ways to upgrade the quality of the internship experience for future interns. Try to be as diplomatic and tactful as possible. Use the four-step approach from Chapter 13 to offer positive feedback as well as specific suggestions for possible improvements. At this time there may also be some mention of an appropriate way to mark the occasion of your leaving. A farewell party or dinner can help everyone on the staff say good-bye.

Interns are also frequently asked to evaluate their internship experiences for the internship seminar or coordinator—to make an oral presentation, a written exercise, or a final entry in their journal, for example. Sometimes these evaluations are filed in the career library or coordinator's office to provide other students with data to evaluate potential internship sites. Typical questions you could be asked to address are:

■ Did you meet your learning objectives? Explain how.

■ What was your most important contribution?

■ In what ways did your internship disappoint you?

■ What new skills did you develop or hone?

■ How did your relationship with your supervisor either help or hinder you in meeting your goals?

■ What were the highlights of your internship?

■ List tips for future interns who select this site.

Consider asking coworkers and supervisors to serve as references for your job search. If you wish to have a letter of recommendation for your file, be sure to mention what sort of position you are seeking as well as a summary of your relevant qualifications. This is where an updated copy of your resume comes in handy. Give your reference writer a definite time line for preparing your letter or filling out your recommendation form; open-ended requests are easy to bury in the "to do" box and ignore.

Case in Point

Brenda was applying for a job at the Mercy Center for the Disabled and needed a letter of recommendation from her former internship supervisor. Brenda had done similar work for Easter Seals where she had interned six months earlier. When Brenda finally got around to contacting her former supervisor, however, the woman had moved to another state and left no forwarding address.

TIP

Establishing a placement file at your college's career services office can help you avoid Brenda's dilemma. Collecting and storing references in a timely and secure way ensures they will be available when needed. Most institutions of higher learning maintain placement files for many years after graduation, subject to updating and reactivation. Maintaining your own reference file at home is another option.

Don't be shy about asking your supervisor or coworkers for names of contacts for networking possibilities and names of organizations that could have entry-level openings in your field. If your supervisor indicates positive feelings about your performance at your internship, he or she might be willing to put in a good word for you with colleagues and friends. Your supervisor could also be a good source of information about additional internships, allowing you to broaden your experience further.

Be sure to write a thank-you letter, either typed or handwritten, to your supervisor to acknowledge his or her efforts on your behalf. (See Example 9 on next page.) While you may say a verbal thank you, written communication is more durable and will help your supervisor recall you and your internship in the years to come.

There are a number of tactful ways to maintain contact with your internship supervisor and coworkers. Send a holiday card. Drop them a postcard while on vacation or when you have relocated. Keep them posted about your academic plans and programs. Call to congratulate staff when you hear about promotions, marriages, and births. Stop in to say hello when you are in town. Cultivate these relationships; you never know when the seeds you have planted in the course of your internship will bear fruit.

(Example 9)
Internship Thank-You Letter

December 4, 1995

112 Varnum Place
Towson, MD 21204

Randall B. Barnes, Director
Mary Clayton Center
Baltimore, MD 21208

Dear Mr. Barnes:

While I am excited about graduation, I am sad about leaving my internship at the Mary Clayton Center. I have enjoyed working with the staff and patients and have learned so much about the challenges that face victims of spinal cord injury. I particularly liked tutoring Edna Johnson and hope that she will be able to get her G.E.D.

I know that training a new intern was a lot of work for you and I appreciate your time and patience in answering all my questions and finding interesting tasks for me to do. I bought two of the books you recommended and will try to continue the learning process on my own.

I have enclosed a copy of my updated resume, which includes my internship experience at the Mary Clayton Center. Any suggestions you might have about my resume or people in the field I could contact about full-time employment would be very welcome.

Thank you again for helping to make my internship a rewarding experience. I will try to keep in touch with you and the rest of the staff.

Sincerely,

Peggy Moran

Enclosure: resume

Communicating the Value of Your Internship

Making the most of your internship opportunity is an ongoing process that extends beyond the day your internship ends. Knowing in your heart how much you have benefitted from an experience isn't enough. Your next step is to update your resume, using compelling language to effectively communicate your improved experience, knowledge, and skills to potential employers.

When it comes to describing their internships on a resume or cover letter, former interns seldom give themselves enough credit for the skills they have learned, developed, or contributed. To avoid overstating their accomplishments, they tend to downplay their skills and achievements. The end result is a resume that lists a lackluster collection of tasks and duties that fail to grab a potential employer's attention. While it is imperative that all information appearing on a resume be factual, don't confuse a powerful presentation and vivid style with exaggerating or misrepresenting the truth.

Interpret your internship experiences in the most positive light possible. Adele Scheele, a nationally recognized career consultant, stresses the importance of positive self-presentation when dealing with potential employers. "If you describe a project you worked on in terms of what you actually did, what you learned, whether it worked, what others did, what others thought about it, and how you would do it again, you control the way you present yourself and give the most positive interpretation of your past and present performance on the job. . . . In this kind of recounting, you are really being asked to sell yourself" (Scheele, p. 7).

Use action labels—words and phrases—to enhance your internship description on your resume, cover letter, or job application. Practice speaking to others about your internship using these terms. It is in your best interest to take Scheele's advice and train yourself to "give a truer and more positive picture" of your skills and accomplishments (Scheele, p. 7).

■ **Itemize and specify** the actions you have taken in the course of your internship. General statements fail to convey the particular actions taken and skills applied. Refer to the action labels list to help you account for all you have done. Don't sacrifice valu– able information in an effort to conserve space.

Case in Point

Joan's resume offered this brief summary of her six-month internship: "Intern, Little Folks Day-Care Center, Philadelphia, PA. Watched children in before-school program on weekdays."

Joan's description of her internship, while accurate and concise, lacked clarity and precision. While it isn't necessary to detail each and every action, Joan could definitely enrich her description by identifying some of the specific skills and actions she took during this six-month period:

■ maintained a safe, creative environment for children
■ selected and taught crafts projects
■ guided games and activities
■ collected fees from parents
■ dispensed medication
■ began a tutoring program

■ **Quantify your actions.** Using numbers in your descriptions will create a vivid picture of your internship activities. Larger numbers can suggest intensity of effort, diligence, and level of accomplishment. Using the qualifiers "up to," "more than," and "approximately" is necessary for accuracy when you must estimate quantities and amounts.

Case in Point

Joan could enhance her action descriptions by inserting numbers:

■ maintained a safe, creative environment for thirty children between ages five and twelve
■ collected more than $2,000 in fees a week
■ began tutoring program involving fourteen children
■ dispensed medication to ten children suffering from attention deficit disorder and diabetes

■ **Describe what you learned** at your internship. Even if your role was limited to observer or gofer, you probably picked up some critical facts and insights that will help you in the future. Summarize these new insights and information on your resume.

Familiarity with a certain working environment may give you an edge over the competition for a future job.

Case in Point

Joan's internship description on her resume should capture some of the things she has learned during her six months at the Little People's Day-Care Center:

- exposed to all aspects of running a before-school care program—administration, budgeting, maintenance, and programming
- interacted with board members, teachers, and parents at monthly board meetings
- learned state and federal legal codes that govern day-care licensure and certification
- worked on solving space limitation problems

Credit your impact and contributions. What added value did you bring to your worksite? How did your actions contribute to the organizational mission? Interns often downplay their role in the internship, reluctant to claim even a small part of the credit for successful team projects or organizational outcomes. If you don't portray yourself as a vital contributor to the organization, however, it will be difficult to persuade future employers to give you a chance to play a key role in their organizations. You can do a good job of self-presentation without playing fast and loose with the truth. Ask yourself what part *you* played in cutting costs, generating revenue, increasing productivity, improving quality, saving time, using technology, coming up with new ideas, and motivating others.

Case in Point

After considering the implications of all her actions at her internship site, Joan decided the addition of contribution statements to her internship description accurately represented what had actually occurred and did not stretch the truth:

- authored marketing letter sent to 750 families in the Keokuk area
- researched drug awareness programs in day-care centers for university professor, resulting in publication of an article in the *Nation's Day-Care Review*

■ assisted in fund-raising drive that raised 25 percent more than in any of the previous five years

Explore all the ramifications of your internship experience. Give yourself credit where credit is due. Provide the most detail about those actions and accomplishments that are relevant to the full-time position you are seeking. Locate related information at the top of your internship description or highlight it so employers will be sure to see it right off the bat. Most important, practice representing yourself in writing and in conversation as the knowledgeable professional you are in the process of becoming.

Use presentation skills to write a vivid account of your internship actions and outcomes without embellishing or exaggerating. Keep in mind the added value you brought to the organization. See if you can incorporate the following action verbs: *increased, saved, created, solved, reduced, sold, transformed, initiated, decreased, improved, changed, built, won, solved,* and *developed.*

_____

_____

_____

_____

_____

_____

Identify the personal traits you honed during your internship stint, such as: *self-reliance, cooperation, versatility*. Give an example of a situation where you demonstrated each quality.

_____

_____

_____

_____

_____

_____

_____

_____

_____

Conclusion

I've never met a student who regretted doing an internship. There are some who wish they could have done multiple internships or those who felt they could have benefitted from better supervision or a different internship track. But for the most part, the internship is a win-win experience for both student and employer, laying the groundwork for successful career development.

Try not to worry about program titles. Real-world work experience—whether it is labelled internship, field experience, volunteer opportunity, summer job, work-study, co-op, or practicum—is what it's all about. Paid or unpaid, credit or not-for-credit, full-time or part-time—related experience will undoubtedly be the critical factor in launching your career. Internships are definitely worth your time.

> The bottom line is that work works. Student employment is in large degree beneficial to the student's academic persistence and attainment as well as to his or her future career success. And not least, an applicant's work experience is often the deciding factor in a recruiter's offering that sought-after entry-level job on the heels of the graduation ceremony.
>
> (Brougham and Casella, p. 55)

Glossary
of Useful Terms

annual report. Summarizes the business and financial activities of an organization.

benefits. May comprise more than 28 percent of total compensation costs; include: social security, pensions, medical benefits, insurance, stock options, profit sharing, tuition assistance, parental leave, etc.

Bureau of Labor Statistics (BLS). Government agency that makes projections about the number, distribution, and composition of jobs in the future.

chief executive officer (CEO), chief financial officer (CFO). Individuals who run large organizations and develop policies that govern the company.

commission. An agreed-upon percentage of sales paid to a salesperson.

Dictionary of Occupational Titles. Contains numbers classifying occupations by type of work, required training, physical demands, and working conditions. Used primarily by state employment services to classify applicants and job openings.

downsizing. Reduction in the number of employees in a business or organization.

entry-level job. Beginning position or grade level in an organization.

Equal Employment Opportunity Act. A federal law to provide equal employment opportunity for all and prohibit discrimination on the grounds of age, race, color, religion, sex, national origin, or physical or mental handicap.

for-profit organizations. Companies operating to earn profits. Pay taxes on earnings. Represent approximately 72 percent of all employers.

government agencies. Include city, county, state, and federal agencies. Represent approximately 18 percent of all employers.

headhunter. Sophisticated employment agency that specializes in a particular industry or type of work. Deals with companies that want experienced employees of high caliber who earn more than $35,000 annually.

interest inventories. Tests to assist individuals with making career decisions, identify areas of interest and curiosity. Examples: SIGI+, *Strong Vocational Interest Inventory*, and *Campbell Interest Skills Survey*.

lead. Name of an organization that might be a potential customer.

mentor. Individual in the workplace with more skills and experience than you who takes you under his or her wing.

mission. The purpose for which the organization was established—its goals.

networking. An informal system used by people who want to improve their chances for advancement or for a better job by establishing or maintaining contact with others who might be helpful.

nonprofit organizations (third sector, not-for-profit, voluntary sector). Organizations involved with work that benefits the public. Usually have tax-exempt status. Run by a board of directors (trustees) who hire an executive director. Represents approximately 10 percent of employers. Examples: associations, philanthropic organizations, religious organizations, human service agencies, and cultural organizations.

organizational chart. Diagram that shows an organization's various job titles and their relationships to each other.

paraprofessional. An occupation that requires some training or formal education and is near or close to another occupation requiring more formal education.

power structure (hierarchy). How power is allocated from the top down in any organization.

privately owned company. Does not trade on stock exchange and is not required to make operating information public.

publicly owned company. Makes shares of stock available for purchase. Financial and other information must be revealed, making these organizations easier to research.

self-assessment. The process of evaluating one's abilities, talents, and personal traits.

skill. The ability to do something well.

staff v. line positions. Employees who make or sell products are line people. Accounting, research, public relations, human resources, and other administrative or support functions are staff positions.

telephone hot lines. Telephone recordings of job listings maintained by organizations.

vendoring out (outsourcing, contracting out). The practice of having an outside vendor provide services that were formerly done by employees within the business.

workers' compensation. An insurance plan that provides compensation for workers injured on the job.

working conditions. The circumstances or situations that make up the surroundings for a worker.

work values. Important priorities and considerations in choosing a job and a workplace.

Bibliography

Berson, Judith. "Helping Hands Win," *Journal of Career Planning and Employment* (Summer 1993), pp. 30–35.

Bloch, Deborah Perlmutter, Ph.D. *How to Have a Winning Job Interview*. Lincolnwood, IL: VGM Career Horizons, 1992.

Bloch, Deborah Perlmutter, Ph.D. *How to Write a Winning Resume*. Lincolnwood, IL: VGM Career Horizons, 1993.

Brooks, Randy. "Observation & Reflection in Internships," NSEE *Quarterly* (Fall 1993), pp. 12–13, 24.

Brougham, Catherine E., and Donald A. Casella. "Student Jobs Open Front Doors to Careers," *Journal of Career Planning and Employment* (Summer 1995), pp. 24–27, 54–55.

Bureau of the Census. "The Other Shoe: Education's Contribution to the Productivity of Establishments Findings," *EQW National Employer Survey* (1995), pp. 1–5.

Digeronimo, Theresa. *A Student Guide to Volunteering.* New Jersey: Career Press, 1995.

Figler, Howard E. *Path, A Career Workbook for Liberal Arts Students.* Cranston, RI: Carroll Press, 1979, pp. 73–77.

Hastings, Michael. "Getting It Together: The Art of the Professional Portfolio," *College Employment Institute Newsletter*, Michigan State University, Career Development and Placement Services (Summer 1995), pp. 1–3.

Kolb, D. A. *Experiential Learning: Experience as the Source of Learning and Development.* Englewood Cliffs, NJ: Prentice Hall, 1984.

Langhorne, Karyn E., and Eric R. Martin. *How to Write Successful Cover Letters.* Lincolnwood, IL: VGM Career Horizons, 1994.

Little, Thomas C. "History and Rationale for Experiential Learning," NSEE *Resource Paper #1* (1982), pp. 1–17.

Lubach, Don, and Deborah Fuller. "Fighting Against the Sexual Harrassment of Interns," *Journal of Career Planning and Employment* (Summer 1992), pp. 29–31.

Marler, Patty, and Jan Bailey Mattia. *Job Interviews Made Easy*. Lincolnwood, IL: VGM Career Horizons, 1995.

Marler, Patty, and Jan Bailey Mattia. *Resumes Made Easy*. Lincolnwood, IL: VGM Career Horizons, 1995.

Martin, Eric, and Karyn E. Langhorne. *Cover Letters They Don't Forget*. Lincolnwood, IL: VGM Career Horizons, 1993.

Moore, David Thornton. "Perspectives on Learning in Internships," *Perspectives on Experiential Education*. Malabar, FL: Krieger Publishing Company, 1992.

Moore, David Thornton. "Students at Work: Identifying Learning Internships," NSEE *Resource Paper #2* (1984).

Provenzano, Steven. *Slam Dunk Resumes*. Lincolnwood, IL: VGM Career Horizons, 1994.

Public Library Association Job and Career Information Services Committee. *The Guide to Basic Cover Letter Writing*. Lincolnwood, IL: VGM Career Horizons, 1995.

Public Library Association Job and Career Information Services Committee. *The Guide to Basic Resume Writing*. Lincolnwood, IL: VGM Career Horizons, 1991.

Rowh, Mark. *Slam Dunk Cover Letters*. Lincolnwood, IL: VGM Career Horizons, 1997.

Scheele, Adele. *Skills for Success*. New York: Ballantine Books, 1979.

Shingleton, John D. *Job Interviewing for College Students*. Lincolnwood, IL: VGM Career Horizons, 1995.

Sweitzer, H. F., and M. A. King. "The Internship Seminar: A Developmental Approach," NSEE *Quarterly* (Fall 1995), pp. 1, 22–25.

Weinstein, Bob. *I'll Work for Free: A Short-Term Strategy for a Long-Term Payoff*. New York: Henry Holt & Company, Inc. (1994), pp. 67–86.

Wutzdorff, Allen. "Service Learning Belongs," *Journal of Career Planning and Employment* (Summer 1993), p. 33.